THE TIMES OF THE GENTILES

by Theodore H. Epp
Director
Back to the Bible Broadcast

A
BACK TO THE BIBLE
PUBLICATION

Back to the Bible
Lincoln, Nebraska 68501

75,000 printed to date—1977
(5-4229—75M—67)
ISBN 0-8474-0716-0

Printed in the United States of America

Foreword

In preparation for a lengthy radio series on the Book of the Revelation, Theodore H. Epp brought a short series on the highlights of the Book of Daniel. The series was not intended to be a detailed study of the Book of Daniel but only a survey of the prophecies that are basic to an understanding of Revelation.

This book contains that short series on the Book of Daniel. It was later printed in the *Good News Broadcaster* and was made available in reprint form. This is the first time, however, that all of the messages have been made available in book form.

May the study of prophecy emphasize to you the urgency of living a pure life that will magnify God and draw others to Him. "Wherefore, beloved, seeing that ye look for such things, be diligent that ye may be found of him in peace, without spot, and blameless" (II Pet. 3:14).

—Harold J. Berry
Personal Assistant
to Theodore H. Epp

Contents

Chapter 1

God Rules

The basic theme of the Book of Daniel is that the most high God rules in the kingdoms of men and gives them to whomever He chooses. The book itself is not a study of isolated experiences but of related accounts concerning God's progressive revelation of future events. But demonstrated again and again is the fact that God is in control of the affairs of men.

The book begins with these words: "In the third year of the reign of Jehoiakim king of Judah came Nebuchadnezzar king of Babylon unto Jerusalem, and besieged it. And the Lord gave Jehoiakim king of Judah into his hand, with part of the vessels of the house of God: which he carried into the land of Shinar to the house of his god; and he brought the vessels into the treasure house of his god" (1:1,2). Note the statement, "The Lord gave . . . into his hand." God was in control.

This marks not only the beginning of the Book of Daniel but also the beginning of what the Bible calls the "Times of the Gentiles." They began in the year 606 B.C. and will end with the Second Coming of Christ as Israel's Messiah.

In Daniel 12 we read that the prophet was instructed to "shut up the words, and seal the book, even to the time of the end" (v. 4). And

7

again in verse 9 he was told: "Go thy way, Daniel: for the words are closed up and sealed till the time of the end." What Daniel presents, therefore, is a record of events, beginning with his day, through the present dispensation of the grace of God and continuing to the coming Tribulation and the time of Christ's Second Coming. This is when He will destroy the kingdom of Antichrist and set up His own millennial kingdom on the earth.

The expression "Times of the Gentiles" is found in the Gospel of Luke. Predicting the destruction of Jerusalem, which occurred in A.D. 70, and the worldwide dispersion of the Israelites, our Lord said, "They shall fall by the edge of the sword, and shall be led away captive into all nations: and Jerusalem shall be trodden down of the Gentiles, until the times of the Gentiles be fulfilled" (Luke 21:24).

The destiny of the Gentile nations is dramatically unfolded in the dream image of Daniel 2, where we are given a panoramic view of Gentile world governments as they are related to Israel. The great image, as seen by Nebuchadnezzar and explained by Daniel, had a head of gold, a breast and arms of silver, a belly and thighs of brass, and legs of iron with feet made partly of iron and partly of clay. Daniel explained the iron-clay portion in these words: "And whereas thou sawest the feet and toes, part of potters' clay, and part of iron, the kingdom shall be divided; but there shall be in it of the strength of the iron, forasmuch as thou sawest the iron mixed with miry clay. And as the toes of the feet were part of iron, and part of clay, so the kingdom shall be partly strong, and partly broken. And whereas thou sawest iron

8

mixed with miry clay, they shall mingle themselves with the seed of men: but they shall not cleave one to another, even as iron is not mixed with clay" (2:41-43).

The two kinds of human government spoken of here are present today. We have dictatorships, but we also have democracies. Though these do not readily form a union, a strong leader is coming who will weld them into a world government for a short period of time.

This great prophecy of Daniel 2 makes it clear that Gentile world dominion from the time of Nebuchadnezzar until Christ's Second Coming will consist of only four world kingdoms. Despite repeated attempts by other nations to become world rulers since the Roman Empire fell, none have succeeded, and none will. The final Gentile empire under the Antichrist will be related in some way to the former Roman Empire. In fact, it is depicted as the ten toes of the image.

There is a fifth kingdom—Christ's kingdom—but it is not a Gentile one. The four Gentile kingdoms are marked by deterioration. Also, the final attempt by the last world Gentile ruler will have only brief success, and then God through Christ will crush all Gentile world powers and establish a righteous government on the earth. This we learn in Daniel 2:44,45: "And in the days of these kings [the ten kings symbolized by the toes of iron and clay] shall the God of heaven set up a kingdom, which shall never be destroyed: and the kingdom shall not be left to other people, but it shall break in pieces and consume all these kingdoms, and it shall stand for ever. Forasmuch as thou sawest that the stone was cut out of the mountain without hands, and that it brake in pieces the iron, the brass, the clay, the silver, and the gold; the great God hath made known to the king what shall come to pass hereafter: and the dream is certain, and the interpretation thereof sure." The wisdom and might of God will be seen by men. The Gentile governments will be destroyed before their eyes.

Daniel reveals that God is enthroned high above the governments of men. He works out His own will through His infinite wisdom and irresistible might. At the present time those who have eyes to see will see evil being allowed to reach its full development, thus warranting its ultimate and complete destruction.

Daniel's visions in chapters 7 and 8 give further insight into God's sovereign power in directing the affairs of His universe, and His purpose to unite all things in Christ. This purpose is stated in Ephesians 1:10: "That in the dispensation of the fulness of times he might gather together in one all things in Christ, both which are in heaven, and which are on earth; even in him."

The kingdoms of the world will become the kingdoms of God as stated in Revelation 11:15: "And the seventh angel sounded; and there were great voices in heaven, saying, The kingdoms of this world are become the kingdoms of our Lord, and of his Christ; and he shall reign for ever and ever."

It is God's purpose that Christ will be made preeminent as stated in Philippians: "Wherefore God also hath highly exalted him, and given him a name which is above every name" (2:9).

God has never given up His sovereign power over the earth. We see only the governments of men because we look at world affairs with human eyes. But Daniel reveals that the government of God constantly controls the whole earth. His sovereignty in establishing rulers is repeated time and again. This is stated explicitly in Daniel 4: "That the living may know that the most High ruleth in the kingdom of men, and giveth it to whomsoever he will, and setteth up over it the basest of men" (v. 17).

Throughout the Book of Daniel, with one exception, God is given the name of *Adonai Elohim*. The word *Adonai* means the "Supreme Sovereign Lord and Master." *Elohim* means "The Mighty," "The Strong One." So when Daniel speaks of God in relation to the nations of the world, he is talking about the almighty, strong, supreme, sovereign Master of all things.

The one exception to this title for God is found in Daniel 9 where the prophet uses the word "Jehovah." During his supplication for his people he used the covenant name of God, the I Am or the Becoming One, the word speaking of God's special relationship to His people Israel. But not once in the three empires in which he served did Daniel speak of God as Jehovah to his Gentile rulers. Daniel always referred to Him by the titles of *Adonai* and *Elohim*.

It was this aspect of God's power among the nations that Daniel declared before Nebuchadnezzar. He said, "Thou, O king art a king of kings: for the God of heaven hath given thee a kingdom, power, and strength, and glory. And wheresoever the children of men dwell, the beasts of the field and the fowls of the heaven hath he given into thine hand, and hath made thee ruler over them all.

11

Thou art this head of gold" (2:37,38). This exalted God to His proper place and was a firm warning to Nebuchadnezzar that he was able to take Jehoiakim, king of Judah, prisoner only because God allowed it.

It is stated at least three times in Daniel 4, making plain the meaning of the tree vision, that God rules in the kingdoms of men and gives these kingdoms to whomever He wills.

In chapter 5 we have the record of Belshazzar's blasphemous feast. It is apparent from the record that Daniel had been in obscurity for a period of time. He was taken out of seclusion to interpret the handwriting that had appeared on the wall in front of the king at this feast. By this time, Daniel was possibly 85 years of age. God used him at this particular time to warn Belshazzar of coming judgment and to explain the reason for the judgment. He told the king that although he was fully aware of what had happened to Nebuchadnezzar, he, Belshazzar, had not humbled his heart but had turned against the Lord of heaven. So God gave the handwriting on the wall to indicate that He was going to depose Belshazzar and establish another king and kingdom.

Only because of Daniel's inspired prophecy do we know the certain outcome of trends in world affairs today. This great prophetic book clearly foresaw and revealed in advance the development of governmental powers, from the absolute monarchy of Nebuchadnezzar, to the principles which have developed into Communism and the nationalism and self-determination characterizing peoples today.

From this same book we learn that knowledge

will increase. There will be a development and spread of what men would call good, and some of these things we enjoy now. But along with the benefits of modern knowledge, we are seeing the increase of evil. Man's evil nature and ways will finally outweigh the benefits brought to modern society through the advancement of science and other phases of man's knowledge. God will finally bring the kingdoms of the Gentiles to an end and establish a new kingdom in righteousness with Christ as King of kings and Lord of lords.

Chapter 2

The Times of the Gentiles

The phrase "Times of the Gentiles" has to do with Gentile world governments as they relate to Israel. As stated in chapter 1, this time began with Nebuchadnezzar's conquest of Jerusalem in 606 B.C. and will end with the Second Coming of Christ.

In Daniel 2 we have the record of Nebuchadnezzar's dream which some have called the ABC of Bible prophecy. It must be studied in connection with, and in preparation for, the study of the Book of the Revelation. That book might be called the XYZ of Bible prophecy or the final consummation of God's program for the Gentiles. The information given is not a complete history of Gentile world governments but records their history as it relates to God's program with the people of Israel.

We might compare the present time in world history to a great stage on which most of a play has already been acted out—only the last act is yet to come. The curtain is still down, but behind it can be heard rumblings and movements as the stage props are being prepared for the last great, dramatic and climactic scene. The wars and rumors of wars, the peace talks and the plans for human survival are all part of the noises we hear, while at the same time the clouds of judgment are

14

gathering. When will the last curtain rise? We are not sure, but Daniel takes us behind that curtain so that we need not be ignorant of what is coming.

The world can only guess and wonder at what is taking place at the present time, and the best that anyone can do is plan for the present and the future. It is the privilege, however, of the Bible-believing student of prophecy to know what events are coming and what the outcome will be.

The Prophet Daniel was one of the advisers of Nebuchadnezzar. It is very evident from what we read in chapter 1 that Daniel was a person of high moral courage. This is emphasized repeatedly throughout the book, for he took his life in his hands many times in order to be faithful and true to his God.

In chapter 2 we have the account of Nebuchadnezzar's dream. The king was awakened from his sleep, startled and alarmed, but could not recall the dream—at least that is what he told his wise men. He asked them to tell him what his dream was and then to interpret it for him. The men immediately protested, saying that he was asking for something that no other king had ever required. They said that only the gods, who were supposedly spirit beings, could reveal such matters. Nebuchadnezzar became angry, accused them of being deceivers, and said they were to give him the information or he would destroy all of them. This included Daniel and his friends.

Apparently Daniel had not been with the wise men when they were summoned by the king, so when he heard of the king's decree, he made his way into Nebuchadnezzar's presence. He asked for time to pray to his God in heaven who, Daniel said,

15

would reveal the information Nebuchadnezzar wanted.

Daniel and his friends prayed, and God revealed to Daniel the dream and the interpretation. Daniel praised God for His wisdom and might because He changes "the times and the seasons: he removeth kings, and setteth up kings: he giveth wisdom unto the wise, and knowledge to them that know understanding: He revealeth the deep and secret things: he knoweth what is in the darkness, and the light dwelleth with him" (2:21,22).

Daniel then went before the king and described to him the great image that he had seen in his dream. Daniel added, "Thou sawest till that a stone was cut out without hands, which smote the image upon his feet that were of iron and clay, and brake them to pieces. Then was the iron, the clay, the brass, the silver, and the gold, broken to pieces together, and became like the chaff of the summer threshingfloors; and the wind carried them away, that no place was found for them: and the stone that smote the image became a great mountain, and filled the whole earth" (vv. 34,35).

Daniel proceeded to give the interpretation of the dream. Nebuchadnezzar was a king of kings, for God had given him a kingdom, power and glory. The Babylonian ruler himself was the head of gold. This marks the beginning of the Times of the Gentiles and identifies the first great world power of the four pictured in the prophetic dream.

Following Nebuchadnezzar, another kingdom, inferior to his kingdom, was to arise—a kingdom symbolized by silver. A third kingdom of brass was to follow which would rule over all the earth. A fourth kingdom was to be as strong as iron: "Forasmuch as iron breaketh in pieces and subdueth all things: and as iron that breaketh all these, shall it break in pieces and bruise" (v. 40).

Sometimes the expression "Times of the Gentiles" is confused with another expression used in the New Testament—"fulness of the Gentiles." This latter expression is used in Romans 11:25, where Paul says, "For I would not, brethren, that ye should be ignorant of this mystery, lest ye should be wise in your own conceits; that blindness in part is happened to Israel, until the fulness of the Gentiles be come in."

The fulness of the Gentiles has to do with the completion of the Body of Jesus Christ, the Church. The calling out of this Body is described for us in Acts 15:14. We learn that God visited "the Gentiles, to take out of them a people for his name." Individual Jews may also turn to Christ, but the Jews as a nation do not come into focus again until God is through calling out those who will make up the Church. When this number is complete, God will take the Church away.

That such is God's program is clear from the words of James as he summed up the discussion in the Jerusalem Council: "And to this agree the words of the prophets; as it is written, After this I will return [after the fulness of the Gentiles is come in], and will build again the tabernacle of David, which is fallen down; and I will build again the ruins thereof, and I will set it up" (vv. 15,16).

This is God's wonderful plan of calling out a born-again people for Himself. Then, following the Tribulation, Christ will return and establish His kingdom over Israel and over the world.

The kingdoms represented in Nebuchadnezzar's dream were progressively inferior from the standpoint of their governmental design. Babylon was an absolute monarchy. This was followed by Medo-Persia, inferior because its kings shared the rulership with others.

The third kingdom was of brass, again inferior to the other two. This was the Grecian Empire, first ruled by Alexander and then divided after his death.

The final kingdom, of iron, though not identified in Daniel, is unmistakably the Roman Empire. This empire was dominant during the Saviour's time on earth and during the later formation and spread of the Church. Rome was inferior to these others in that its government was further removed than any of them from an absolute monarchy.

This fourth Gentile kingdom is represented by two legs of iron. This clearly identifies it as Rome, which became divided into eastern and western sections. Looking back from our vantage point in history, we see how clearly this prophecy has been fulfilled. Only one part of this great prophecy still awaits fulfillment—that involving the ten toes composed of iron and clay.

This Roman kingdom, as already noted, was originally divided into two parts, but the final division spoken of in verses 41-43 involves many parts. The feet and toes have to do with the last form of the fourth kingdom, which is actually an extension of the old Roman Empire. Politically, the Roman Empire has been extinct for many centuries, but from its ruins will rise the federation of nations that is prophesied here. Some will be strong, some weak, but together they will form a

18

powerful kingdom for a time. This will be the last great Gentile dominion before Christ's kingdom is established on the earth.

There has been no world kingdom since Rome. The barbarians who came into Rome from the north did not become a world power. In the seventh century, the Arabs attempted to rule the world, but they, too, failed. In more recent times, men such as Napoleon, the Kaiser, Hitler and Mussolini all tried but failed to become world rulers. At the present time, international Communism is attempting to dominate the earth, but this, too, is doomed to failure. Russia will make a great bid for power during the Tribulation but will fail completely, according to Ezekiel 38 and 39. Prophesied events are beginning to take place again in the Mediterranean countries and the Middle East.

In God's mind absolute monarchy is the perfect form of government. Men, however, have demonstrated that it is impossible for them to achieve this goal. The imperfection lies in them. Only the perfect Son of God will form and maintain a perfect government. Man, because of sin, self and Satan, will never reach this goal.

The last attempt at such a world government by the Gentiles is the one pictured by the ten toes. It will be a confederation of ten kingdoms, or nations, ruled by the Antichrist. It is very possible that fear of atomic destruction will play a vital role in their union.

Though the metals in the image decrease in value, from the gold down to the iron, at the same time they increase in strength. Silver is stronger than gold and brass stronger than silver, and iron is the strongest of all. Thus the kingdoms are pictured as increasing in brute strength but becoming inferior in governmental structure.

The final Gentile kingdom, this confederation with its elements of strength and weakness, will form a very fragile government and will not last long. God has the last word. The fifth kingdom of Nebuchadnezzar's dream image is not a man-made kingdom but one of divine origin.

A stone is cut out without hands and strikes the image on the feet and breaks it to pieces. The various parts of the image become like the chaff of the summer threshing floors, which the wind carries away. The stone that smites the image becomes a great mountain and fills the whole earth (Dan. 2:35).

In the days of those last kings of the confederation, God will establish His kingdom through His Son. There is no need to guess who is involved, for the stone cut out without hands is Christ, whose birth was supernatural. He was virgin born. He had no human father.

Throughout the Old and New Testaments the Lord Jesus is symbolized as a stone or rock. Psalm 118:22-24 says: "The stone which the builders refused is become the head stone of the corner. This is the Lord's doing; it is marvellous in our eyes. This is the day which the Lord hath made; we will rejoice and be glad in it." Christ is the rock on which the Church is built, according to Matthew 16. Peter, in his first epistle, describes Christ as the "chief corner stone, elect, precious" (2:6).

There are several different descriptions of the stone in Scripture. First, there is Christ the smitten rock, prophetic of His crucifixion and the fact that from Him would flow life for all who would drink (I Cor. 10:4; Ex. 17:6). To the Church, He is the foundation and chief cornerstone (Eph. 2:19,20). To the Israelites, He was a stumbling stone at His first coming (Rom. 9:31-33). They could not accept Him because He did not come as they thought He should. But to Israel at His Second Coming He will be the headstone of the corner. To the Gentile world power, He will be a striking stone who will destroy all the kingdoms of the world (Dan. 2:34).

In the divine purpose, the stone which will destroy the kingdoms of men will grow and fill the whole earth. He will be to unbelievers a crushing stone of judgment, but to believers a stone of rejoicing. The time when the stone will smite the feet of the image is yet future—it will take place at the end of the Tribulation.

Nothing in this prophecy supports the idea that the gradual spreading of the gospel through the centuries will bring the world to faith in the Lord, as some interpret this passage. It will take divine force to destroy the governments of men. Following that judgment Christ will establish His kingdom. His kingdom will not be brought in by peaceful means but by sudden judgment.

Chapter 3

Nebuchadnezzar's Image of Gold

What do we keep our eyes on these days? Are they on the many troubles that are plaguing the earth? Or are we looking to Him who rules in heaven and earth? As we have stated, one of the great outstanding truths in the Book of Daniel and also in the Book of the Revelation is that the God who lives in the heavens, rules on the earth. He gives men authority in the governments of the world as He chooses.

In the third chapter of Daniel we find that Nebuchadnezzar, who had been designated as the head of gold, had set up a huge image of gold which was to be worshiped: "Nebuchadnezzar the king made an image of gold, whose height was threescore cubits, and the breadth thereof six cubits: he set it up in the plain of Dura, in the province of Babylon" (v. 1). Evidently, Nebuchadnezzar was not satisfied with being designated as the "head of gold," so he made an actual image of gold. He then commanded all the nations over which he ruled to worship the image. He was determined to be everything to those people. He was going to be their god as well as their political ruler.

We are not sure how much time elapsed between the events of chapter 2 and chapter 3 of Daniel; it could have been from 10 to 20 years.

The amount of time involved is not as important as the direction of Nebuchadnezzar's thoughts during that time.

Babylon was known for being not only a political system but also a religious one. It was opposed to God and was Satan's counterfeit of the kingdom that God promised would one day appear on this earth. A type of the Babylonian religious system is still with us today.

Nebuchadnezzar built the great image of gold, 90 feet high and 9 feet wide, and demanded worship by all in order to unify the religions of the world under himself. These different peoples were to send their representatives to a sort of dedication service where everyone would be compelled to worship the image on pain of death.

Attempts to unify the religions of the world have been going on ever since that time. Satan has introduced his counterfeit at different periods in the world's history. All of these attempts have had one thing in common—an intense hatred of God's ancient people, the Jews.

The hatred for God's chosen people showed up at this great dedicatory service to the gold image. Some of Nebuchadnezzar's leading men lost no time in reporting that three young Hebrews had refused to bow to the idol. These leaders described them as "Jews whom thou hast set over the affairs of the province of Babylon" (v. 12). And of them they said, "These men, O king, have not regarded thee: they serve not thy gods, nor worship the golden image which thou hast set up" (v. 12).

This particular display of hatred undoubtedly stemmed from the time when Daniel and his three friends were given prominent places in the administration of Nebuchadnezzar's government. In the tests that were given for the high positions to be filled, these Jews stood out as brilliant students. It was evident that God's blessing was on them and Nebuchadnezzar was glad to have such men under him. But their very abilities and their high position made them targets for the jealousy and hatred of their fellow officers.

The prophetic picture revealed in the 3rd chapter of Daniel points to the time known as the Tribulation. During that time, the Antichrist will pollute the Jewish temple in Jerusalem by setting up his image to be worshiped. This is what the Bible calls the "abomination of desolation" (Matt. 24:15)—the desecration of the Jewish temple by the beast. At this time, he will demand that the world worship him.

In his madness at the end time man will again, as did Nimrod (see Gen. 10:8-10; 11:1-9), make every effort to create a world political federation, a world religious federation and a world language in government. Contributing directly to the religious goal, and possibly indirectly to the others, is the ecumenical movement of the present day.

The image in Daniel 3 and the image spoken of in Revelation 13, though separated by at least two and a half millennia, share the common purpose of establishing a universal religion. All through these intervening years there has been a war between God and Satan, between the seed of the woman and the seed of the serpent (see Gen. 3:15). It is not by mere chance that the ecumenical movement of today is seeking to gather all religions into one.

There are several noteworthy matters in the third chapter of Daniel. What we see there shows

24

up again in different ways in the Book of the Revelation. In Daniel we read that three young Hebrew men were thrown into a fiery furnace because they refused to bow to the image of Nebuchadnezzar. They would not join in the united world religion. So the furnace is a type or picture of the Tribulation spoken of in the Book of the Revelation. Nebuchadnezzar illustrates the beast, or the Antichrist, of Revelation 13. The image is a picture of the "abomination of desolation," spoken of first by Daniel (9:27), then by our Lord Himself (Matt. 24:15), and then in the Book of the Revelation (19:20). The three Hebrew men are a picture of Israel in that period known as "the Time of Jacob's Trouble" or "the Tribulation."

The deliverance from the furnace pictures the future deliverance and the exaltation by God of His chosen people, Israel. The men who threw the three Hebrews into the furnace were themselves consumed by the heat of the flames (Dan. 3:22). The furnace had been heated to seven times its normal heat, yet the three Hebrews escaped while their persecutors were destroyed.

This is similar to what God has revealed concerning the terrible Tribulation. The persecution against Israel during that time will be "seven times hotter" than the world has ever experienced before. The enemies of God will try to destroy His ancient people but will fail. God will intervene and deliver them in accordance with His promise to Abraham: "And I will bless them that bless thee, and curse him that curseth thee" (Gen. 12:3).

The confidence in God that the young men of Daniel 3 had is refreshing. We read: "Shadrach,

Meshach, and Abed-nego, answered and said to the king, O Nebuchadnezzar, we are not careful to answer thee in this matter" (Dan. 3:16). That is, they did not need to answer him in that particular matter. Then they continued: "If it be so, our God whom we serve is able to deliver us from the burning fiery furnace, and he will deliver us out of thine hand, O king. But if not, be it known unto thee, O king, that we will not serve thy gods, nor worship the golden image which thou hast set up" (vv. 17,18). Their answer to Nebuchadnezzar's demands was that God was able to deliver them under every condition.

Similar to this is Hebrews 7:25: "Wherefore he is able also to save them to the uttermost that come unto God by him, seeing he ever liveth to make intercession for them." Also assuring is Hebrews 2:18: "For in that he himself hath suffered being tempted, he is able to succour [help] them that are tempted." Jude 1:24 comforts us: "Now unto him that is able to keep you from falling, and to present you faultless before the presence of his glory with exceeding joy." Ephesians 3:20 says, "Now unto him that is able to do exceeding abundantly above all that we ask or think, according to the power that worketh in us." This same radiant confidence in God is reflected in Paul's second letter to Timothy: "For the which cause I also suffer these things: nevertheless I am not ashamed: for I know whom I have believed, and am persuaded that he is able to keep that which I have committed unto him against that day" (II Tim. 1:12).

The three Hebrew young men were not only confident that God was able to deliver them, they were also sure that he would deliver them. This is the difference between what we might call "doctrinal acquiescence," or believing that God is able, and a living, active faith, or having confidence that He will deliver. It is the difference between theory and practice.

These three witnesses were not very concerned about whether or not they would be delivered from the furnace, but they were sure that they would be delivered out of the hands of the king. They had yielded their bodies to God and were ready for whatever He called on them to face. Even Nebuchadnezzar admitted this and was forced to admire them. He declared: "Blessed be the God of Shadrach, Meshach, and Abed-nego, who hath sent his angel, and delivered his servants that trusted in him, and have changed the king's word, and yielded their bodies, that they might not serve nor worship any god, except their own God" (Dan. 3:28). Have we thus yielded ourselves to God?

Chapter 4

A Mad Monarch

We are now living near the close of the Times of the Gentiles. Does the term "Times of the Gentiles" mean that God has turned over the affairs of this world to Gentile rulers with no interference on His part? The fourth chapter of Daniel gives a very clear answer to this question. The events recorded there are history to us, but they show how God ruled in the past and will rule again in the future. In fact, Daniel's statement concerning God in chapter 2 shows that God had never relinquished His rulership in the universe and in the world. Daniel spoke of God as the God of heaven who changes the times and the seasons, who removes kings and sets up kings, who gives wisdom to the wise and knowledge to those who want understanding. The events recorded in chapter 4 took place so that men would know "that the most High ruleth in the kingdom of men, and giveth it to whomsoever he will" (Dan. 4:25).

The fourth chapter of Daniel was written by Nebuchadnezzar himself (under the inspiration of God). It relates an experience which taught the king that, in the final analysis, it is God who raises men to be kings and governors. The opening words are "Nebuchadnezzar the king, unto all people, nations, and languages, that dwell in all the earth; Peace be multiplied unto you. I thought it good to shew the signs and wonders that the high God hath wrought toward me. How great are his signs! and how mighty are his wonders! His kingdom is an everlasting kingdom, and his dominion is from generation to generation" (4:1-3).

This is the introduction to a most remarkable experience that Nebuchadnezzar passed through. Chapter 3 shows what heights his pride caused him to reach for, but chapter 4 shows how God brought him back to the reality of being a mere man, dependent on God for his life and position.

The king had a dream that troubled him. He called his astrologers and wise men together to interpret the dream for him, but they did not do so. It does not say they *could* not, but they *did* not. The reason for this was probably that they guessed the true meaning, which was that Nebuchadnezzar was to be humbled, and they were not about to risk their lives by telling him so. It took a man like Daniel, a man of God and a man of high moral courage, to kindly, yet frankly, tell Nebuchadnezzar the truth.

In his dream Nebuchadnezzar saw a great tree which was strong; it reached to heaven and was seen all over the earth. It provided food and shelter for all flesh. Then a holy one came down from heaven and said, "Hew down the tree, and cut off his branches, shake off his leaves, and scatter his fruit: let the beasts get away from under it, and the fowls from his branches: nevertheless leave the stump of his roots in the earth, even with a band of iron and brass, in the tender grass of the field; and let it be wet with the dew of heaven, and let his portion be with the beasts in the grass of the earth: let his heart be changed from man's, and let a beast's heart be given unto him; and let seven times pass over him" (vv. 14-16).

The reason for cutting down the tree is also given: "This matter is by the decree of the watchers, and the demand by the word of the holy ones: to the intent that the living may know that the most High ruleth in the kingdom of men, and giveth it to whomsoever he will, and setteth up over it the basest of men" (v. 17).

Following this, Daniel gave the interpretation. The prophet, being careful how he delivered this ominous message, said, "My lord, the dream be to them that hate thee, and the interpretation thereof to thine enemies" (v. 19). Daniel was saying that he wished what was going to happen to Nebuchadnezzar was going to happen to Nebuchadnezzar's enemies instead. Then the prophet told the king that the great tree represented the king himself. He had become so great that his dominion reached to the end of the earth.

The vision of the watcher, or holy one, coming down from heaven and commanding that the tree be cut down, represented a judgment that was to come on Nebuchadnezzar: "They shall drive thee from men, and thy dwelling shall be with the beasts of the field, and they shall make thee to eat grass as oxen, and they shall wet thee with the dew of heaven, and seven times shall pass over thee, till thou know that the most High ruleth in the kingdom of men, and giveth it to whomsoever he will" (v. 25). Because of his pride and evil deeds, Nebuchadnezzar was going to be deposed and driven from the fellowship of men and would have to live like an animal for seven years. But at the end of that time he was to be restored. Daniel said,

"And whereas they commanded to leave the stump of the tree roots; thy kingdom shall be sure unto thee, after that thou shalt have known that the heavens do rule" (v. 26).

Daniel did not stop with this prophecy of the king's restoration but admonished him, assuring him of the possibility that such a judgment would not fall if he changed his ways. Even though Nebuchadnezzar was a man of the world, Daniel loved him and sought God's best for him. Here is what the prophet said: "Wherefore, O king, let my counsel be acceptable unto thee, and break off thy sins by righteousness, and thine iniquities by shewing mercy to the poor; if it may be a lengthening of thy tranquillity" (v. 27). But Nebuchadnezzar did not mend his ways for very long. At the end of 12 months he looked over his city and became filled with pride because of it. Three or four chariots could drive abreast on top of its walls. It had enough arable land within it for its inhabitants to raise all their own food. He had married a princess who longed for something to remind her of the mountains where she had been raised. She was unhappy with the flat, level country in and around Babylon. To please her, he built tall, vaulted buildings, covered them with earth, and planted trees and gardens. These home-made "mountains" became one of the seven wonders of the ancient world—the Hanging Gardens of Babylon. So as he looked over this large city, the pride of his heart caused Nebuchadnezzar to say, "Is not this great Babylon, that I have built for the house of the kingdom by the might of my power, and for the honour of my majesty?" (v. 30).

Pride was the king's downfall. Daniel 3 told of the 90-foot image made of gold that Nebuchadnezzar had erected, apparently for the purpose of self-deification. Now he took credit for all the power and glory that he saw in Babylon. God had no place in his thoughts.

It was then that God spoke: "While the word was in the king's mouth, there fell a voice from heaven, saying, O king Nebuchadnezzar, to thee it is spoken; The kingdom is departed from thee. And they shall drive thee from men, and thy dwelling shall be with the beasts of the field: they shall make thee to eat grass as oxen, and seven times [years] shall pass over thee, until thou know that the most High ruleth in the kingdom of men, and giveth it to whomsoever he will" (vv. 31,32).

The judgment was actual and literal: "The same hour was the thing fulfilled upon Nebuchadnezzar: and he was driven from men, and did eat grass as oxen, and his body was wet with the dew of heaven, till his hairs were grown like eagles' feathers, and his nails like birds' claws" (v. 33).

The restoration of Nebuchadnezzar was also just as God said it would be. "And at the end of the days I Nebuchadnezzar lifted up mine eyes unto heaven, and mine understanding returned unto me, and I blessed the most High, and I praised and honoured him that liveth for ever, whose dominion is an everlasting dominion, and his kingdom is from generation to generation: And all the inhabitants of the earth are reputed as nothing: and he doeth according to his will in the army of heaven, and among the inhabitants of the earth: and none can stay his hand, or say unto him, What doest thou? At the same time my reason returned unto me; and for the glory of my kingdom, mine honour and brightness returned unto me; and my counsellors and my lords sought unto me; and I was established in my kingdom, and excellent majesty was added unto me. Now I Nebuchadnezzar praise and extol and honour the King of heaven, all whose works are truth, and his ways judgment: and those that walk in pride he is able to abase" (vv. 34-37).

Nebuchadnezzar was a man who could speak with the authority of experience. He had seen in himself what God would do to a man who continued to be proud, as though the honors he held were the result of his own abilities and work. He was the head of gold, but only because God had made him so.

Nebuchadnezzar's dream was a prediction of what would happen to him as a result of his pride and unbelief. The judgment fell just as God said it would—this was the historical fulfillment of the dream. But there is a prophetic aspect of Nebuchadnezzar's judgment that goes beyond our own day. The seven years of Nebuchadnezzar's insanity foreshadow the beastiality and corruption of the kingdom of the Antichrist at the end of the Gentile age. The seven-year Tribulation, which will follow the catching away of the Church, will be a time of trouble such as the world has never seen before. Revelation 13, for example, covers this period and lists some of the things that will go on then. The lesson to be learned by the nations will be the same as that learned by Nebuchadnezzar.

The future Tribulation of seven years may well be called the folly, the insanity or the madness of the nations of the earth. They are even now refusing to recognize the God of heaven and are boasting of their achievements as though man were everything and God nothing. This is true also of the so-called Christian nations. Some of them speak of Him, but do not really acknowledge His power and seek His fellowship. But the time of trouble that is coming will eventually change all of that.

When the peoples of the world cry, "Peace and safety," then sudden destruction will fall on them (I Thess. 5:3). They will think they have everything under their control, but they will find their foundations crumbling. God will remove His restraints and man will almost succeed in annihilating himself. In fact, if it were not for the intervention of God, no one would be saved during the Tribulation, according to our Saviour (Matt. 24:22). This fear is gripping people everywhere today. Men have terrible weapons with which to wage war, and so the nations sit in dread of each other.

But God's people do not need to be afraid. This time of trouble will happen during the Tribulation. God is holding back the full expression of evil until the fulness of the Gentiles comes, when the Church will be ushered into the presence of Christ. But because of this time of increasing world chaos, we have many opportunities to send forth the gospel of the Lord Jesus Christ.

The Apostle Paul wrote in Romans 13:1: "Let every soul be subject unto the higher powers. For there is no power but of God: the powers that be are ordained of God." The writer of Proverbs 16 makes an astounding statement concerning the same matter: "The Lord hath made all things for himself: yea, even the wicked for the day of evil" (v. 4). We may not completely understand this verse, but we do know Who rules the earth. No wonder Paul, in contemplating the power and majesty of God, said, "How fathomless the depths of God's resources, wisdom, and knowledge! How unsearchable His decisions, and how mysterious His methods! For who has ever understood the thoughts of the Lord, or has ever been His adviser? Or who has ever advanced God anything to have Him pay him back? For from Him everything comes, through Him everything lives, and for Him everything exists. Glory to Him forever! Amen" (Rom. 11:33-36, *Williams*).

Daniel 4 tells us that God sets over nations the basest, or lowest, of men. The men who are raised to these high positions do not think this of themselves. They often have very high opinions of their own abilities and characters. It is God who says many of them are the lowest of men.

Alexander the Great had a very high opinion of himself. He was a remarkable leader and general but only because God used him to fulfill certain of His purposes in the world. This man dragged himself to a disgraceful early death at the age of 33. He could rule armies, but he could not rule his own appetites. He died at the end of a heavy drinking bout. Few men baser than Nero have been raised to positions of leadership. He was bestial in his conduct and appetites. In more recent history, men like Napoleon, Hitler, Mussolini and Stalin have occupied positions of leadership. Where could we find lower men?

We need to recognize that we are living near the time when the tree of world power will be cut

35

down. The nations of the world are proud; many of them are even denying the existence of God. Like the psalmist we cry, "O Lord, how long?" (Ps. 6:3).

The efforts of many statesmen today to bring about a better understanding among nations is undoubtedly very sincere. Their efforts to bring the nations into closer working harmony may be well-meaning. Men are hoping to bring security and prosperity and peace to a world that has experienced one war after another since the dawn of history. But have we noticed how little or nothing is said of God in all of these plans? He is completely ignored. Some countries may begin their government sessions with prayer, as has been done in the United States, but for the most part God is left out.

The world fears that international destruction is ahead. And certainly, from the standpoint of prophecy, conditions in the seven years of the Tribulation will be worse than anything the world has ever seen before. But these things will be brought to an end. Christ will come and destroy wicked nations that have plagued the earth for so long. He will set up His own kingdom in righteousness and peace.

Daniel 4:34-37 records Nebuchadnezzar's own admission of guilt before God. It tells of his own spiritual change or conversion. This prefigures the conversion of certain Gentiles living during the Tribulation period. Just as Nebuchadnezzar acknowledged the God of Jacob, so will those Gentiles who are referred to as sheep in Matthew 25 in connection with the judgment of the living nations (actually Gentiles). Israel will be restored to her land as the head of the nations, while the converted Gentiles occupy the world around them.

Christ will be preeminent. Every knee will bow before Him. He has been given a name which is above every name so that every knee will bow to Him to the glory of God the Father (Phil. 2:10,11).

Another passage to consider is Zechariah 8:20-23: "Thus saith the Lord of hosts; It shall yet come to pass, that there shall come people, and the inhabitants of many cities: and the inhabitants of one city shall go to another, saying, Let us go speedily to pray before the Lord, and to seek the Lord of hosts: I will go also. Yea, many people and strong nations shall come to seek the Lord of hosts in Jerusalem, and to pray before the Lord. Thus saith the Lord of hosts; In those days it shall come to pass, that ten men shall take hold out of all languages of the nations, even shall take hold of the skirt of him that is a Jew, saying, We will go with you: for we have heard that God is with you."

Thus we see that a world revival and conversion is foreshadowed in the fourth chapter of Daniel. This will take place after the Tribulation, however, and not before. At the present time the Lord Jesus is working in the world to take out a people for His name (see Acts 15:14).

Chapter 5

Deposing a World Ruler

The fifth chapter of Daniel deals with another remarkable event in God's handling of the Gentile nations. This chapter records the end of the Babylonian Empire and the beginning of the reign of the Medo-Persians.

Many years had gone by since Nebuchadnezzar had called on the nations to worship God. Some 70 years had passed since Daniel had been taken as a 14-year-old boy from his home in Judah to the Babylonian court. He was probably about 85 years of age when the events recorded in this chapter took place.

Belshazzar, grandson of Nebuchadnezzar, was in charge of Babylon in the absence of his father. Having seen how God had dealt with his father and particularly with his grandfather before him, Belshazzar was not ignorant of the lessons Nebuchadnezzar had learned from the hand of God. Belshazzar, however, was haughty and rebellious. He had been elevated to a very high position in the kingdom due to the fact that God sometimes exalts men of low character.

Babylon had been besieged by the Medes and Persians for some time. Apparently this gave Belshazzar no anxious moments, for he knew his city was well fortified. It had high, thick walls and was considered completely safe. The inhabitants could grow their own food within the walls and were prepared for a 20-year siege if necessary.

A moat or canal surrounded the city, and the River Euphrates flowed through the city under its walls. Great gates barred any alien force from using the river as a means of entrance into the city.

The Babylonian ruler defied the armies of the Medes and Persians. He showed his contempt for them and lack of fear by throwing a great feast for his generals. About a thousand of his lords were present, and wine flowed freely. As the orgies were reaching their peak, the king told his servants to bring the golden vessels that had been taken from the house of the Lord in Jerusalem. It was while he and his princes, his wives and his concubines drank from these sacred vessels, praising the Babylonian gods and defying Almighty God, that the handwriting appeared on the wall.

More than a century before this event, God had foretold through Isaiah the prophet that Cyrus the Persian would conquer the city of Babylon: "Thus saith the Lord to his anointed, to Cyrus, whose right hand I have holden, to subdue nations before him; and I will loose the loins of kings, to open before him the two leaved gates; and the gates shall not be shut; I will go before thee, and make the crooked places straight: I will break in pieces the gates of brass, and cut in sunder the bars of iron: And I will give thee the treasures of darkness, and hidden riches of secret places, that thou mayest know that I, the Lord, which call thee by thy name, am the God of Israel" (Isa. 45:1-3).

In Isaiah 44 God explained how He was going to use Cyrus to aid in the rebuilding of Jerusalem and the temple there. God called Cyrus His servant because, even though Cyrus was a Gentile and not a believer as far as we know, God used him to carry out His will. And God elevated him to the throne.

God had promised Abraham that those who blessed the Israelites would be blessed, and those who cursed them would be cursed. Some of this blessing and cursing was tied in with the holy things God had entrusted to Israel. Belshazzar still held the Israelites in captivity and had taken the holy things of the temple that had been sanctified for use in that place and defiled them. Therefore, God had to send judgment. The king had touched that which was holy.

The same principle also holds true for us. When we misuse that which is holy to God, we can expect judgment to follow. Our bodies belong to Him. They have been bought with a price and separated for His use (I Cor. 6:19,20). We are not our own.

This principle will also hold true for the future. In the Tribulation when unclean hands are laid on the people and the sacred things of God, the wicked will be judged. Hitler was quickly judged when he tried to destroy God's ancient people. Today, Russia is trying to gain control of the Mediterranean and to unite the Arab nations in an attempt to drive Israel out of existence. When she tries to lay her hands on God's people, that will be Russia's end.

In the same way, when the Antichrist defiles the temple of God, he will soon be brought to an end. God is not mocked. Whatever a man sows, he will also reap (see Gal. 6:7).

Belshazzar had no excuse for what he did. He should have learned from Nebuchadnezzar's experience. He must have seen or at least been told how God had humbled him. But Belshazzar was stubborn and rebellious, honoring his gods and defying Almighty God.

While the Babylonian monarch was persisting in his wicked course, the Persians were diverting the water of the Euphrates, which flowed through the city of Babylon (possibly by using the moat which circled the outside wall), so they could enter the city by walking on the bed of the river. The gates that ordinarily were closed to prevent intruders from entering the city by way of the river were left open that night, just as God had said they would be through His Prophet Isaiah.

Belshazzar's cup of sin was full. Seventy years had passed since Nebuchadnezzar had taken the first captives from Judah into Babylon. The great prophecy of Jeremiah was now to be fulfilled. One of the initial steps was the downfall of the Babylonians and the elevating of the Medes and Persians.

Concerning a day that will come, perhaps in the near future, Joel wrote: "I will also gather all nations, and will bring them down into the valley of Jehoshaphat, and will plead with them there for my people and for my heritage Israel, whom they have scattered among the nations, and parted my land" (Joel 3:2). Our generation has parted the land of Israel—they now live in only a small portion of what God said will eventually belong to them.

While Belshazzar defied God, the handwriting of judgment appeared on the wall. Men cannot defy God and expect to escape the consequences.

When will the cup of iniquity be full for our

nation or for the whole world or for any of us personally? Will God give America up to judgment? The handwriting is on the wall for the world. Why should we think that we can escape? There is a point beyond which God will not allow any of us to go. According to Ezekiel 38 and 39, Russia will seal her own doom when she comes into Palestine in an attempt to take over that land and destroy the Israelites.

God's judgment on the world will not be withheld forever. There is an urgency about these words in Psalm 9: "The wicked shall be turned into hell, and all the nations that forget God. For the needy shall not always be forgotten: the expectation of the poor shall not perish for ever. Arise, O Lord; let not man prevail: let the heathen be judged in thy sight. Put them in fear, O Lord: that the nations may know themselves to be but men" (vv. 17-20).

Belshazzar found that God would not let a man go beyond a certain point. When the drunken orgy was at its height, a hand appeared and wrote on a wall of the palace. Belshazzar was so shocked and filled with fear that he trembled. His limbs shook and his knees knocked. He called for his wise men to interpret the writing, but they could make nothing of it. Then Daniel was sent for, and he was promised an honored place in the kingdom if he would but interpret the message for Belshazzar.

Daniel looked at the man making such great promises to him and told him to offer his gifts to someone else. Though the courage and straightforward talk of this prophet of God might have cost him his life, Daniel knew he had nothing to lose since God was for him.

First he rebuked the king. Daniel reminded him of how Nebuchadnezzar was humbled, yet Belshazzar had learned nothing for himself from his grandfather's experiences. The prophet then went on to interpret the handwriting which read, "Mene, Mene, Tekel, Upharsin" (Dan. 5:25). Daniel said, "This is the interpretation of the thing: Mene; God hath numbered thy kingdom, and finished it" (v. 26). Every moment, every day, every year of Belshazzar's life and Belshazzar's kingdom had been marked. It was all known to God. According to Psalm 139:16, God even knows all about us before we are born, so it is no wonder that Moses asked God, "Teach us to number our days, that we may apply our hearts unto wisdom" (Ps. 90:12). Belshazzar had come to the end of the line. He had triggered the judgment that marked the end of his course.

The word "Tekel" means "weighed." Belshazzar's life was weighed in the scales of God's absolute, righteous judgment. In I Samuel 2:3 we read: "For the Lord is a God of knowledge, and by him actions are weighed." Our actions, motives, thoughts, words—all are weighed as to their exact value by God.

The word "Upharsin" means "divided." This reminds us again of the principle stated repeatedly in the Book of Daniel—that God rules in the kingdoms of men and raises or deposes kings according to His own will. Belshazzar's reign was ended. The Medes and Persians were in the process of taking over the kingdom.

Gentile governments as a whole are beginning to run out of time. It may not be long before the Antichrist appears on the earth and organizes the last great phase of the Times of the Gentiles. He may, for a short time, bring peace and prosperity to the nations, but as soon as he tries to destroy the Promised Land and its people, God's judgment will fall.

Concerning that judgment we read in Matthew 24: "For as the lightning cometh out of the east, and shineth even unto the west; so shall also the coming of the Son of man be. For wheresoever the carcase is, there will the eagles be gathered together. . . . And then shall appear the sign of the Son of man in heaven" (vv. 27,28,30). In Revelation 6 we read that the very surface of the earth is going to be distorted and changed and that men in all stations of life will hide themselves in the dens, rocks and mountains with the hope of hiding from the wrath of the Lamb (vv. 12-17).

In Revelation 19:11-16 we learn that the heavens will be opened and Christ will come leading the armies of heaven and bringing an end to wickedness on the earth. Then He will establish His own kingdom in righteousness and peace.

Chapter 6

Lions' Dens: Past, Present and Future

Most of us are familiar with Daniel's imprisonment and deliverance from the lions' den. Many valuable spiritual lessons can be learned from this event, particularly with regard to Daniel's own faithfulness, integrity, courage and prayerfulness. However, this chapter also contains prophetic truth concerning Israel.

Daniel in the lions' den is a picture or type of the faithful remnant among the Israelites who will be saved in the Tribulation. They will be saved in, not from, that time of trouble that is to come on this earth. Just as Daniel was thrown into the lions' den and saved from any harm while he was there, a certain portion of Israel will be kept safe from harm throughout the judgments and terrible conditions that will exist during the Tribulation. God, who shut the mouths of the lions in Daniel's day and sent His angel to protect the prophet, will protect a remnant of Israelites in the time of trial and sorrow that Jeremiah calls "Jacob's trouble" (Jer. 30:7).

We read about this remnant in Revelation 7:1-4: "And after these things I saw four angels standing on the four corners of the earth, holding the four winds of the earth, that the wind should not blow on the earth, nor on the sea, nor on any tree. And I saw another angel ascending from the

45

east, having the seal of the living God: and he cried with a loud voice to the four angels, to whom it was given to hurt the earth and the sea, saying, Hurt not the earth, neither the sea, nor the trees, till we have sealed the servants of our God in their foreheads. And I heard the number of them which were sealed: and there were sealed an hundred and forty and four thousand of all the tribes of the children of Israel." Twelve thousand persons from each of the 12 tribes will thus be preserved during the Tribulation just as Daniel was saved in the lions' den.

In contrast to this, the born-again Christians of this age, who are members of the Church, the Body of Christ, will not experience the Tribulation at all. Revelation 3:10 says, "Because thou hast kept the word of my patience, I also will keep thee from the hour of temptation [the Tribulation], which shall come upon all the world, to try them that dwell upon the earth." God promises to keep born-again believers of this age from that period. They will not be allowed to go into it. Thus, the Church will be saved from the hour of Tribulation, but Israel will be saved in, or through, the Tribulation.

The experience of Noah is an excellent illustration of this. Noah was saved in, or through, the great flood. He was safe in the ark that passed through the flood, but he was not removed from the earth in order to escape the flood. He was kept safe in the midst of it. This will be the experience of the faithful remnant of Israel in that future seven-year judgment.

Another parallel between the sealed of the Tribulation and Daniel is found in the description given of the remnant in Revelation 14:5. There we

46

are told that no guile was found in their mouths, for they were without fault before the throne of God. This does not mean they were sinlessly perfect, but they were righteous before God. They were saved and therefore were declared righteous through faith in Christ. The same thing was true of Daniel. It is remarkable that the Book of Daniel mentions no fault of his. No blemish of character, no deceit, no sin of any kind is mentioned. He did identify himself with his people Israel and confess his as well as their sin as a nation. But he trusted God and therefore was declared righteous.

This truth is not limited to the 144,000 and Daniel. Any person who trusts in Christ will have his sins forgiven. Nothing is charged against the person who is in Christ Jesus.

A third point of likeness between Daniel and the remnant in the Tribulation concerns the fact that Daniel did not receive a scratch in the lions' den. Daniel stated: "My God hath sent his angel, and hath shut the lions' mouths, that they have not hurt me: forasmuch as before him innocency was found in me; and also before thee, O king, have I done no hurt. Then was the king exceeding glad for him, and commanded that they should take Daniel up out of the den. So Daniel was taken up out of the den, and no manner of hurt was found upon him, because he believed in his God" (6:22,23). This will also be true of the 144,000. They will pass through the Tribulation without harm. They will be divinely protected all the way through.

Another significant factor is that the men who had plotted Daniel's death were themselves destroyed. We read in verse 24: "And the king commanded, and they brought those men which had accused Daniel, and they cast them into the den of lions, them, their children, and their wives; and the lions had the mastery of them, and brake all their bones in pieces or ever they came at the bottom of the den." This is a significant contrast to the remarkable safety Daniel enjoyed. The lions were furious and vicious in their destruction of Daniel's enemies.

During the Tribulation, judgment will fall on those nations and individuals who have persecuted God's people. Jesus said to such people, "Depart from me, ye cursed, into everlasting fire, prepared for the devil and his angels: for I was an hungred, and ye gave me no meat: I was thirsty, and ye gave me no drink: I was a stranger, and ye took me not in: naked, and ye clothed me not: sick, and in prison, and ye visited me not. Then shall they also answer him, saying, Lord, when saw we thee an hungred, or athirst, or a stranger, or naked, or sick, or in prison, and did not minister unto thee? Then shall he answer them, saying, Verily I say unto you, Inasmuch as ye did it not to one of the least of these, ye did it not to me. And these shall go away into everlasting punishment: but the righteous into life eternal" (Matt. 25:41-46).

God said to Abraham: "And I will bless them that bless thee, and curse him that curseth thee: and in thee shall all families of the earth be blessed" (Gen. 12:3). This was no idle promise. God has kept it down through the centuries and will use it as one of His principles of judgment in the Tribulation.

Concerning Israel, God also said, "Let people serve thee, and nations bow down to thee: be lord over thy brethren, and let thy mother's sons bow down to thee: cursed be every one that curseth thee, and blessed be he that blesseth thee" (Gen. 27:29). This same principle is stated again in Deuteronomy 30:7: "And the Lord thy God will put all these curses upon thine enemies, and on them that hate thee, which persecuted thee."

Isaiah repeated similar truth when he wrote: "For the Lord will have mercy on Jacob, and will yet choose Israel, and set them in their own land: and the strangers shall be joined with them, and they shall cleave to the house of Jacob. And the people shall take them, and bring them to their place: and the house of Israel shall possess them in the land of the Lord for servants and handmaids: and they shall take them captives, whose captives they were; and they shall rule over their oppressors" (14:1,2).

God meant what He said when He promised blessing to those who blessed Israel and judgment to those who oppressed His people.

We might say that Israel has passed through many "dens of lions" in the course of its history. God has taken the nation through them and destroyed its enemies in them. Babylon, which persecuted the Jews, was destroyed. Amalek, which tried to exterminate God's Chosen People, is no longer a nation. The Canaanites, early enemies of Israel, were destroyed. Pagan Rome, which persecuted Israel, was destroyed. In our own century, Hitler, who tried to wipe the Jews off the face of the earth, was destroyed. No weapon used against God's ancient people will succeed. Nations today that are boasting of what they will do against the Jews are only laying the groundwork for their own future judgment.

Equally true has been the blessing on those who have blessed Israel. In these last centuries both Britain and the United States have been havens for God's ancient people. Though there is much sin in both nations, and though they will eventually suffer for these things, it is very possible that their present preservation is due in part to the kindness shown to the people of Israel.

God keeps His promises. If we want His blessing, we must obey His instructions found in His Word.

Chapter 7

The Little Horn

Daniel 7 and 8 record a series of visions God gave to His prophet concerning the four great Gentile world empires as they related to the people of Israel. As we have seen, Daniel 2 contains the account of Nebuchadnezzar's dream image of the Times of the Gentiles. The four kingdoms seen in both chapters are the same; they are viewed from different perspectives. Nebuchadnezzar saw them represented by a figure of a man. In Daniel 7 they are presented as four great beasts, each different from the others.

Daniel said, "I saw in my vision by night, and, behold, the four winds of the heaven strove upon the great sea" (v. 2). Four seas are mentioned in the Bible which have played an important part in Israel's history—the Red Sea, the Sea of Galilee, the Dead Sea and the Mediterranean Sea. When the word "sea" is used symbolically, it means "nations." Thus, the action of the four winds of heaven on the great sea would indicate turmoil among the nations which have the Mediterranean as their center. Palestine itself is the center of biblical history and the place on earth to which Christ will return.

The interpretation of Daniel's vision begins with verse 17: "These great beasts, which are four, are four kings, which shall arise out of the earth."

51

Kings obviously represent kingdoms, so there is no problem in recognizing that the four kingdoms of Nebuchadnezzar's dream image and the four beast kingdoms of Daniel's vision are the same.

The first beast is compared to a lion which "had eagle's wings" (v. 4). This first kingdom is Babylon, which was still in existence at the time Daniel had his vision (v. 1). This corresponds to the gold portion of the image seen by Nebuchadnezzar, as recorded in Daniel 2:38.

The second beast is like a bear: "And behold another beast, a second, like to a bear, and it raised up itself on one side, and it had three ribs in the mouth of it between the teeth of it: and they said thus unto it, Arise, devour much flesh" (7:5). The kingdom described here was the Medo-Persian Empire, which had a huge and very destructive army. This corresponds to the silver part of the image seen by Nebuchadnezzar (2:32).

The third kingdom is described as follows: "After this I beheld, and lo another, like a leopard, which had upon the back of it four wings of a fowl; the beast had also four heads; and dominion was given to it" (7:6). This beast corresponds to the kingdom of brass in Daniel 2:39 and symbolizes Greece, which became a world power under Alexander the Great. The wings represent the swiftness of Alexander's conquests. He was a world ruler by the time he reached his early thirties. When he died at the age of 33, his kingdom was divided among four of his generals. This fact was prophesied in the figure of the four heads.

The fourth beast was the fiercest of all. "Behold a fourth beast, dreadful and terrible, and strong exceedingly; and it had great iron teeth: it devoured and brake in pieces, and stamped the residue with the feet of it: and it was diverse from all the beasts that were before it; and it had ten horns" (7:7). This corresponds to the iron kingdom of Daniel 2:40-43.

The prophet paid special attention to the horns and said, "I considered the horns, and, behold, there came up among them another little horn, before whom there were three of the first horns plucked up by the roots: and, behold, in this horn were eyes like the eyes of man, and a mouth speaking great things" (7:8).

There is no question about the meaning of this part of the vision. Daniel was told: "And the ten horns out of this kingdom are ten kings that shall arise: and another shall rise after them; and he shall be diverse from the first, and he shall subdue three kings" (v. 24). The rest of the Book of Daniel has a great deal to say about this little horn which represents the Antichrist. The Book of the Revelation also gives us a good deal of information about him. His appearance has not been revealed, but he will come out of a confederation of ten nations located in the general geographical area of the old Roman Empire.

The fourth kingdom will continue until it is replaced by the kingdom of Christ. This, too, is in keeping with the dream image of Nebuchadnezzar (Dan. 2:44,45).

The Book of the Revelation also deals with the future aspect of the Roman Empire. A key chapter on this subject is Revelation 13. There we are told of a beast coming up out of the sea, having seven heads and ten horns. One of these heads is described as being wounded to death; then the deadly wound is healed. This undoubtedly refers to one of the nations that now seems to be in oblivion but will be revived and take a prominent place in the end time. Such a political revival may seem impossible at the present time, but the Word of God is sure. A great political power will arise in the area of the Mediterranean Sea, and its appearance will startle the world. Furthermore, this political power will be controlled by a man who is described in the Bible as the "man of sin" (II Thess. 2:3). He is the Antichrist, the little horn of Daniel 7. His power will be extensive—he will gain control of the confederation of ten nations described in both Daniel and Revelation.

This man of great evil will unite these nations, bringing order out of disorder and peace out of threatened war. For a brief time he will bring to the earth the longed-for rest and prosperity the nations desire. But they will soon be disillusioned, and the time of peace they hoped for will not come through the little horn, the Antichrist.

The first appearance of the man of sin on the world scene will be insignificant, but he will soon gain control of the world. In Revelation 6 he is pictured as riding on a white horse, thus imitating Christ. A bow will be given to him, but he will have no arrows. He will conquer, but it will be done through subtlety. He will sit at peace tables and make promises and use every method possible to deceive the nations. For a time the world will think that he has the real solution for its problems. It will not take him long to gain control of the ten nations that will be in the area of the Mediterranean.

54

In Revelation 6:4 we find that the same man will take peace from the earth. In the same chapter we learn that, as the rider on the black horse, he will bring famine on the earth (vv. 5,6). Famine logically follows war conditions. The rider on the fourth horse in this chapter represents the same man bringing widespread death to the nations (vv. 7,8).

A further description of the little horn, or the man of sin, in Daniel 7 is that he speaks great things and that his "look was more stout than his fellows" (v. 20).

The little horn will make war against the saints of God (v. 21). Further explanation of this is given in Revelation 13. There we learn that the false prophet will demand that everyone on earth worship the Antichrist, and those who refuse will be put to death. The mark of the beast will be required before a person can buy or sell. To refuse the mark will result in starvation (vv. 15-17).

Paul, in writing about the Antichrist, described him as one "who opposeth and exalteth himself above all that is called God, or that is worshipped; so that he as God sitteth in the temple of God, shewing himself that he is God" (II Thess. 2:4).

In Daniel 7:25 we learn that the little horn will "wear out the saints of the most High." The words "wear out" are the translation of a word that refers to mental affliction, not bodily affliction. We see some of this today, in Communism, which uses brainwashing as part of its technique to enslave people.

The horn will also "think to change times and laws" (Dan. 7:25). The Book of the Revelation points out that he will reorganize all aspects of human existence on an entirely new and different basis designed to erase the memory of the past. He will create a new beginning with himself as the god of the people. The changing of times and laws has no reference to the Law of Moses. That was given to the Jewish people primarily, not to the nations of the world. The times and laws referred to here are fundamental, basic conditions of all human society. An example of one of those basic principles of living is the headship of the man over the woman. The principle was clearly established in Genesis 2. It does not make woman man's slave, but it does place the responsibility for the household on the shoulders of the man.

Another basic principle he will try to destroy is the law of marriage that was given in Genesis 2:24. Marriage is for one man and one woman, a relationship which only death can break. Divorce was not even considered. It was the basic truth our Saviour pointed to when He was asked about divorce. He pointed back to the beginning and said, "[God] made them male and female, ... For this cause shall a man leave father and mother, and shall cleave to his wife: and they twain shall be one flesh. ... What therefore God hath joined together, let not man put asunder" (Matt. 19:4-6).

God's Word clearly emphasizes the necessity of the substitutionary atonement for man's sin. Christianity alone, of all the religions in the world, requires man's faith in Christ as the basis for salvation. All the others have human works as their bases. These two completely opposite systems are illustrated in the fourth chapter of Genesis in the offerings brought by Cain and Abel. Throughout history Satan has been trying to foist his system on the world; thus when the little horn or the Antichrist comes, he will command the world to worship only him.

Another principle for human government laid down in the Book of Genesis concerns capital punishment. God said, "Whoso sheddeth man's blood, by man shall his blood be shed: for in the image of God made he man" (Gen. 9:6). This principle was established by God, but it is the subject of hot debate by man today.

Another basic law or principle is the seven-day week with one day for rest. This is being increasingly violated. Here again the Antichrist will try to change things to suit his own program.

It is a cause for thanksgiving that this evil person will not reign very long on the earth. We read in Daniel 7:25 that his power will last "until a time and times and the dividing of time." The word "time" in this context means a year. The smallest number of "times" would be two, and a "half a time" would be a half year. So this man will have power for three and a half years. God will stop him short, for God is sovereign. Verse 26 says, "But the judgment shall sit, and they shall take away his dominion, to consume and to destroy it unto the end." The power that will strip the Antichrist of his rule will be the Son of Man, Christ Himself, who will come "with the clouds of heaven" (Dan. 7:13,14). He will also be accompanied by the saints of the most high God, who will take the kingdom and possess it forever under his leadership (7:18).

Two different groups are referred to as saints in the Scriptures. One group is made up of the members of Christ's Body, the Church, and are identified as such in I Corinthians 6:2. There Paul says that "the saints shall judge the world" and that these saints are God's people of today. This statement agrees with the promise to the Church in Revelation 2:26,27: "And he that overcometh, and keepeth my works unto the end, to him will I give power over the nations: and he shall rule them with a rod of iron; as the vessels of a potter shall they be broken to shivers: even as I received of my Father."

However, the Church is not spoken of in Daniel. The saints spoken of there are the Old Testament saints, or the believing Israelites. The kingdom, rather than judgment, will be given to the restored people of Israel.

Geographical Origin of Antichrist

Where will the Antichrist come from? This question is answered in the eighth chapter of Daniel. There Daniel relates his vision of the ram and the male goat. For a while nothing could withstand the power of the ram; then the male goat came and, in the fury of his power, destroyed the ram. The goat had a great horn between his eyes, but the horn was finally broken and four other horns arose in its place. Then out of one of these four came a little horn which became strong in the south, in the east and in the land of Palestine itself. This horn increased in power, even over the host of heaven, and "cast down some of the host and of the stars to the ground, and stamped upon them" (v. 10). This little horn magnified himself "even to the prince of the host, and by him the daily sacrifice was taken away, and the place of his sanctuary was cast down" (v. 11).

The interpretation of this vision discloses that the ram symbolizes Medo-Persia and the male goat the Grecian Empire (vv. 20,21). Then we are told, "And in the latter time of their kingdom, when the transgressors are come to the full, a king of fierce countenance, and understanding dark sentences, shall stand up" (v. 23). We know from history that this prophecy was fulfilled in Antiochus Epiphanes, who came from the Syrian division of the Grecian Empire about 170 B.C.

There is actually a double prophecy here with a double fulfillment. The first prophecy and fulfillment had to do with Antiochus who, during his short reign, captured Jerusalem and defiled the temple by offering a pig on the altar and setting himself up as God. His power lasted for about three and a half years.

Antiochus prefigured in his character and actions the coming Antichrist—the little horn of Daniel 7. The coming of the Antichrist will be the fulfillment of the second aspect of this prophecy.

Antiochus came from Syria. This area was later controlled by Rome, and it is very possible that the Antichrist will also come from that particular locality. We cannot be dogmatic about this point, but Antiochus Epiphanes and the coming Antichrist do have a number of characteristics in common.

Chapter 8

God's Timetable for Israel

The ninth chapter of Daniel is a key chapter in the whole prophetic program of God. The first 19 verses concern Daniel's prayer and confession. The last part of the chapter deals with the answer to Daniel's prayer that God sent to him through the angel Gabriel. And it is this portion, verses 20-27, which is the skeleton, or framework, of all prophecy. It is the general outline around which all prophecy is built. So if we err in our understanding of the 70 weeks of Daniel, we will misunderstand other prophetic truth. But if we correctly understand the message given, then we will be able to fit related prophecies of other portions of the Bible into the framework provided here.

While Daniel was speaking, praying, confessing his own sins and the sins of his people, Israel, and presenting his supplication before the Lord, Gabriel came and touched him "about the time of the evening oblation" (vv. 20,21).

The first thing Gabriel said to Daniel was, "O Daniel, I am now come forth to give thee skill and understanding" (v. 22). There was to be no guessing about the information which was to be given to Daniel. When Daniel began to pray and intercede for his people, God commanded Gabriel to carry His Word to Daniel. When the angel came, he said, "I am come to shew thee; for thou art greatly beloved: therefore understand the matter, and consider the vision" (v. 23). The information given was to clearly explain the great events of the future.

The actual prophecy begins in verse 24: "Seventy weeks are determined upon thy people and upon thy holy city, to finish the transgression, and to make an end of sins, and to make reconciliation for iniquity, and to bring in everlasting righteousness, and to seal up the vision and prophecy, and to anoint the most Holy [place]."

A fixed period of time was determined for the people of Israel and Jerusalem. The word "determined" means "fixed"—something that cannot be changed. It was decreed by God, not by men. When God decrees a plan or a program, it cannot be changed.

The program involved Daniel's people, Israel, and their holy city, Jerusalem. Daniel had been praying for these—his people and Jerusalem. It would be unscriptural, therefore, to apply this prophecy to any other group or city.

The word translated "weeks" is *shabua*, meaning, literally, a "seven." So the passage should be read, "Seventy sevens are determined." The word does not refer to a week of days, as it does in English.

The Jews used the number seven to refer to days, but they also used it to refer to years. The land was to be tilled for 6 years, and then it was to rest the 7th, or Sabbath, year (Lev. 25:3,4). After 49 years, which included 7 Sabbaths of years, was the year of Jubilee. It was the 50th year and was a very important one in Israel's social life.

Certainly weeks of days were not referred to in Daniel's prophecy because there would have been only a little over a year involved, or exactly 490 days. This would not have allowed nearly enough time for the city to be rebuilt and destroyed and for the other events of verse 24 to be fulfilled.

The word *shabua* is found in only one other passage in Daniel: "In those days I Daniel was mourning three full weeks. I ate no pleasant bread, neither came flesh nor wine in my mouth, neither did I anoint myself at all, till three whole weeks were fulfilled" (10:2,3). Here Daniel fasted three full weeks, or literally, "three sevens of days." Had days been meant in Daniel 9, the same Hebrew construction would have been used. Therefore, the weeks of Daniel 9:24-27 refer to sevens of years, which equals 70 times 7 years, or 490 years.

When did Daniel's 490-year period begin? The answer is given in verse 25: "Know therefore and understand, that from the going forth of the commandment to restore and to build Jerusalem unto the Messiah the Prince shall be seven weeks, and threescore and two weeks." This totals 69 weeks, or 483 years. The beginning, however, was dated from when the commandment to restore and to build Jerusalem was given.

This commandment is recorded in the Book of Nehemiah. Nehemiah was deeply concerned over a report from Jerusalem that the Jews in that city were in great distress, that the city's walls were broken down, and that its gates had been burned. Nehemiah could not keep his sorrow from showing on his face as he served as cupbearer before Artaxerxes, the king. The Persian monarch wanted to know what had brought sadness to his servant, so Nehemiah told him of the condition of Jerusalem.

This took place in the month of Nisan (which falls during March and April on our calendar) in the 20th year of Artaxerxes. The king asked what he might do to help the situation. Nehemiah requested a leave of absence and permission to rebuild Jerusalem's walls. This was granted. The decree is stated in part in Nehemiah 2:8: "And a letter unto Asaph the keeper of the king's forest, that he may give me timber to make beams for the gates of the palace which appertained to the house, and for the wall of the city, and for the house that I shall enter into. And the king granted me, according to the good hand of my God upon me." This, then, was the decree that marked the beginning of Daniel's prophecy.

Prior to this action by Artaxerxes, three decrees had been made on behalf of the people of Israel by two different kings. The Israelites were given permission to return to Jerusalem and to rebuild the temple. However, no permission had been given to rebuild the walls, which would have made it a fortified city once again. The permission to return and rebuild the temple was given by Cyrus, king of the Medes and Persians (II Chron. 36:22,23; Ezra 1:1-4). This same decree was confirmed by Darius, who was also of the Medes and Persians (Ezra 6:1-12).

A second similar decree was made by Artaxerxes (Ezra 7:11-26). But as far as building was concerned, permission was given regarding the temple only, until Nehemiah made his request to rebuild the city.

Notice the six specific things that were to be

accomplished during Daniel's prophecy of 490 years. The first three concern the removal of Israel's national sin. (It is important to differentiate between individual and national sins.) The last three involve the establishment of righteousness in Israel.

The first goal for this 490-year timetable is the most important. It is summed up in the words "to finish the transgression" (Dan. 9:24). This answered Daniel's prayer of confession. He had asked for God's forgiveness of Israel, because as a nation they had rejected God and had followed idols. God's answer was that He would finish this transgression. In other words, He would bring an end to the national apostasy.

Second, God purposed to "make an end of sins" (v. 24)—to restrain or seal up the deliberate wickedness of Israel. Further explanation is given in Ezekiel 37:23: "Neither shall they defile themselves any more with their idols, nor with their detestable things, nor with any of their transgressions: but I will save them out of all their dwellingplaces, wherein they have sinned, and will cleanse them: so shall they be my people, and I will be their God."

Third, God's purpose for the 490 years was to make "reconciliation for iniquity" (Dan. 9:24). This was also provision for Israel's national guilt. Today, any individual Israelite can have his sins forgiven through Jesus Christ. God is no respecter of persons. In his great sermon at Pentecost, Peter said, "For the promise is unto you [Israelites], and to your children, and to all that are afar off, even as many as the Lord our God shall call" (Acts 2:39). This call is not only for the Jews but also for the Gentiles. Forgiveness is available for any individual Jew at any time for all his sins.

However, Daniel's prophecy emphasizes the fact that, during the 490-year period, God would make provision for reconciliation of Israel's national iniquity. Paul referred to this in Romans 11:25,26: "For I would not, brethren, that ye should be ignorant of this mystery, lest ye should be wise in your own conceits; that blindness in part is happened to Israel, until the fulness of the Gentiles be come in. And so all Israel shall be saved: as it is written, There shall come out of Sion the Deliverer, and shall turn away ungodliness from Jacob."

Zechariah wrote of this also: "And I will pour upon the house of David, and upon the inhabitants of Jerusalem, the spirit of grace and of supplications: and they shall look upon me whom they have pierced, and they shall mourn for him, as one mourneth for his only son, and shall be in bitterness for him, as one that is in bitterness for his firstborn" (12:10). Zechariah 13:1 speaks of the same matter: "In that day there shall be a fountain opened to the house of David and to the inhabitants of Jerusalem for sin and for uncleanness."

The fourth purpose of the 70 weeks of Daniel was to "bring in everlasting righteousness" (Dan. 9:24). This will involve a new covenant with Israel and Judah. Concerning this, Jeremiah 31 says, "Behold, the days come, saith the Lord, that I will make a new covenant with the house of Israel, and with the house of Judah: not according to the covenant that I made with their fathers in the day that I took them by the hand to bring them out of the land of Egypt; which my covenant they brake, although I was an husband unto them, saith the Lord: but this shall be the covenant that I will make with the house of Israel; After those days, saith the Lord, I will put my law in their inward parts, and write it in their hearts; and will be their God, and they shall be my people" (vv. 31-33).

The fifth purpose was "to seal up the vision and prophecy" (Dan. 9:24). In other words, God would vindicate the truth of the visions that had been given and establish the authenticity of the prophets by the literal fulfillment of their prophecies.

The sixth purpose of the 490 years was "to anoint the most Holy" (v. 24). Translated literally, this means "the most holy place." It does not refer to Christ as a person, but to the reestablishing of the Holy of Holies, which in the old temple was the habitation of God among His people. The glory of God left that old temple some 2500 years ago, but this relationship will be established once again. Undoubtedly this is connected with Christ's return and the establishing of His throne on earth.

Two temples related to Israel's future are spoken of. One of these may be built very soon, but it will later be desecrated by the Antichrist. Then a second temple will be built during the kingdom of Christ on earth. This temple is described in Ezekiel 40-42.

Major Divisions in the 490-Year Period

Some of the major divisions in this period are given in Daniel 9:25,26: "Know therefore and understand, that from the going forth of the commandment to restore and to build Jerusalem unto the Messiah the Prince shall be seven weeks, and threescore and two weeks: the street shall be built again, and the wall, even in troublous times. And after threescore and two weeks shall Messiah be cut off, but not for himself."

These weeks, you will remember, are weeks of years, and according to the Jewish calendar, they have 360 days each. The period began in the month of March, 445 B.C. "Seven weeks" are actually 49 years. Verse 25 indicates that Jerusalem was rebuilt during a time of trouble and violence. From the end of the 49 years until Messiah the Prince was another period of "threescore and two weeks," or 434 years. These two periods of 49 and 434 years total 483 years.

On April 6, A.D. 32, the 483 years came to a close. On that very day the Lord Jesus Christ, Messiah the Prince, was hailed by the people of Israel under that title. The Triumphal Entry of our Lord into Jerusalem, which we celebrate as Palm Sunday, fulfilled to the day the 483 years from the time Artaxerxes gave the commandment to Nehemiah to restore and to build Jerusalem. Within the next few days the Messiah was crucified.

Concerning our Lord's Triumphal Entry, the Prophet Zechariah stated: "Rejoice greatly, O daughter of Zion; shout, O daughter of Jerusalem: behold, thy King cometh unto thee: he is just, and having salvation; lowly, and riding upon an ass, and upon a colt the foal of an ass" (9:9).

Luke's Gospel records the event as follows: "And when he was come nigh, even now at the descent of the mount of Olives, the whole

67

multitude of the disciples began to rejoice and praise God with a loud voice for all the mighty works that they had seen; saying, Blessed be the King that cometh in the name of the Lord: peace in heaven, and glory in the highest" (19:37,38). But this joyful greeting was only temporary. The leaders of the people were opposed to the Lord and soon turned the hearts of the multitude against Him.

Aware of what was coming, the Lord wept over Jerusalem: "And when he was come near, he beheld the city, and wept over it, saying, If thou hadst known, even thou, at least in this thy day, the things which belong unto thy peace! But now they are hid from thine eyes" (vv. 41,42).

The nation as a whole did not realize the significance of the events taking place before them. Christ first had to come as their Saviour before He could become their King. All this was hidden from most of the people. They could not see that Jesus was their Messiah. Four days after His Triumphal Entry into Jerusalem, Jesus was crucified. He was cut off, but not for Himself—He died for a lost world.

Seven years of Daniel's prophecy have not been fulfilled. The "countdown" stopped at the death of Christ, and an undetermined period will pass before the rest of the prophecy is fulfilled.

We are now living in the dispensation of the Church, a time during which "blindness in part is happened to Israel, until the fulness of the Gentiles be come in" (Rom. 11:25). James tells us that at the present time God is calling out a people for His name, and after this program is ended God will establish the earthly kingdom once again (Acts 15:14-18).

The period in which we are now living is not mentioned in Daniel, though time is left for it. It is during this unspecified length of time that the things of Daniel 9:26 take place. "And the people of the prince that shall come shall destroy the city and the sanctuary." This took place in A.D. 70 when the Romans, under the leadership of Titus, destroyed Jerusalem and the temple.

Look again at the expression "the people of the prince that shall come." Since it was the Romans who came in A.D. 70, it will be from this same area that another prince, a wicked person, will come. The Antichrist is referred to here, and this provides us with further confirmation that he will come from an area that was formerly part of the old Roman Empire.

The nation of Israel is referred to when it says, "The end thereof shall be with a flood, and unto the end of the war desolations are determined" (9:26). Israel was scattered among the nations in that judgment of the first century A.D., and the people formed themselves into a nation again in 1948. They face severe persecution in the years ahead.

The Lord Jesus warned in Matthew 24:6,7 that wars and rumors of wars would come on the earth. But His people were not to be troubled, because these things must happen before the end comes. He went on to predict, "For nation shall rise against nation, and kingdom against kingdom: and there shall be famines, and pestilences, and earthquakes, in divers places" (v. 7). This refers in particular to the Tribulation, when the Antichrist will take peace from the earth. Jeremiah's words clarify this: "Alas! for that day is great, so that none is like it: it is even the time of Jacob's trouble, but he shall be saved out of it" (30:7). This is the final "week" or seven-year period of Daniel's prophecy.

Another very significant event related to that last seven-year period is foretold in Daniel 9:27. Of the prince that will come, the Antichrist, we learn: "And he shall confirm the covenant with many [Israel] for one week [a seven-year period]: and in the midst of the week he shall cause the sacrifice and the oblation to cease, and for the overspreading of abominations he shall make it desolate, even until the consummation, and that determined shall be poured upon the desolate."

The Antichrist will make a covenant with the people of Israel in which he will promise to be their protector. After three and a half years, he will break this covenant with very serious results for Israel and for himself, because his power will eventually be broken. A period of unparalleled suffering and judgment will come on the earth so that God's purposes, which He has before determined, may be fully completed.

Chapter 9

Events in the End Time

The Bible clearly sets forth the details concerning the great Battle of Armageddon—where it will be fought, when it will be fought, and what nations will be involved. In an examination of these matters, Daniel 11 is a key chapter of the Bible.

The first 35 verses of Daniel 11 are now history. They cover the period from Darius the Mede to the deceitful and blasphemous words and actions of Antiochus Epiphanes. Antiochus Epiphanes was not a notable man in world history but he was in Israel's history. Bible prophecy does not concern itself with world or Gentile history as such but only with history as it affected Israel and the Holy Land.

During the time of Antiochus Epiphanes, the Israelites who truly knew God were able to accomplish many notable feats. Daniel 11:33 says, "The teachers among the people shall cause many to gain insight, but for many days they shall be downed by sword and flame, prison and plunder" (*Berkeley*).

Daniel 11:35, which is a bridge between the historical material in the chapter and the information concerning the future Antichrist, says, "On the part of some teachers their stumbling shall be for their refinement and purification to make

71

them white, preparatory to the final period which is delayed until the appointed time" (*Berkeley*). This verse introduces the last part of Daniel 11, which describes the last 7 years of the 490-year period of Daniel's vision (9:20-27).

Describing the last seven years of his prophecy, or the time commonly known as the "Tribulation," Daniel said, "And the king shall do according to his will; and he shall exalt himself, and magnify himself above every god, and shall speak marvellous things against the God of gods, and shall prosper till the indignation be accomplished: for that that is determined shall be done" (11:36). This same truth is emphasized in II Thessalonians 2, which tells of the sudden appearance of the Antichrist on the world scene: "Let no man deceive you by any means: for that day shall not come, except there come a falling away first, and that man of sin be revealed, the son of perdition; who opposeth and exalteth himself above all that is called God, or that is worshipped; so that he as God sitteth in the temple of God, shewing himself that he is God" (vv. 3,4). At the present time, however, "the mystery of iniquity doth already work: only he who now letteth [hinders] will let [hinder], until he be taken out of the way [at the Rapture of the Church when believers who are indwelt by Christ will be caught up to heaven]. And then shall that Wicked [one] be revealed, whom the Lord shall consume with the spirit of his mouth, and shall destroy with the brightness of his coming" (vv. 7,8). This wicked person, the Antichrist, will create increasing havoc in the world during the seven years of the Tribulation.

Our Saviour was in obscurity for 30 years until His baptism; then His brief ministry began. Undoubtedly, the Antichrist will try to imitate Christ even in this respect. The Antichrist may even be on the earth now, though members of the Body of Christ will not see him, since the Church will be removed before he is revealed.

In almost every way, the Antichrist is opposite to the Lord Jesus Christ. The Antichrist will be a self-willed person, in contrast to Christ, who came not to do His own will but to please the Father. The Antichrist will seek personal benefits, whereas Christ came not to be ministered to, but to minister.

The Antichrist will magnify himself above every god—even above the God of the Bible. His speech will be blasphemous, and he will prosper until God calls him to account. He will gain the confidence of the world by presenting a "foolproof" plan for peace. He will gain Israel's support by offering to protect them against their enemies.

Daniel 11:37,38 present the Antichrist as an apostate from some form of Christianity, not of the nation Israel: "Neither shall he regard the God of his fathers, nor the desire of women, nor regard any god: for he shall magnify himself above all. But in his estate shall he honour the God of forces: and a god whom his fathers knew not shall he honour with gold, and silver, and with precious stones, and pleasant things."

How the Antichrist Will Work

Verses 39-45 of Daniel 11 give a detailed account of how the Antichrist will strive to reach his goals. These verses also explain what conditions will be like during the Tribulation.

Verse 39 says: "With devotees of a strange god he will man the fortified strongholds; on those who acknowledge him he will bestow great honor; he shall make them rulers over many and will apportion the land to them" (*Berkeley*). Another translation of this verse is, "And he shall deal with the strongest fortresses by the help of a foreign god. Those who acknowledge him he shall magnify with glory and honor, and he shall cause them to rule over many, and shall divide the land for a price" (*Amplified*).

The Antichrist will use flattery and will spend great sums of money. He will divide the land of Israel among those who support him. However, this division of the land will be his fatal mistake. By attacking Israel and this nation's land, the Antichrist will be challenging God Himself. God will then step into the picture and allow him to go no further.

At the beginning of the 70th Week of Daniel, the Antichrist will confirm a covenant with Israel (9:27). In the middle of the week, or after three and a half years, the Antichrist will break his covenant and will defile the temple by setting up his image in it to be worshiped. He will set himself up as God and divide Israel's land among his favorite followers.

Then we are told in Daniel 11:40: "And at the time of the end shall the king of the south push at him: and the king of the north shall come against him like a whirlwind, with chariots, and with horsemen, and with many ships; and he shall enter into the countries, and shall overflow and pass over." The expression "the time of the end" is very important. This no doubt coincides with the second seal of Revelation 6:3,4, when war breaks out during the first half of the Tribulation.

A large buildup for the final battle of Armageddon will occur during the second half of the Tribulation. Where will this war of Armageddon be fought? It involves a much larger territory than many have thought. Revelation 16:14-16 tells us, "For they are the spirits of devils, working miracles, which go forth unto the kings of the earth and of the whole world, to gather them to the battle of that great day of God Almighty. Behold, I come as a thief. Blessed is he that watcheth, and keepeth his garments, lest he walk naked, and they see his shame. And he gathered them together into a place called in the Hebrew tongue Armageddon." Verse 16 is the only verse in the New Testament that uses the name "Armageddon," although the same location is referred to many other times in Scripture.

Some of the confusion about the Battle of Armageddon has resulted from some of the ways it has been identified. Some Bible students believe that it will be fought when the Russians come down from the north against Palestine. Others say the battle will take place when the forces against God come from the south. Still others identify it as the battle to be fought when the kings of the East come against the Holy Land. Yet the Bible indicates that the enemies of God will come from all directions in their opposition and hostility to the Lord. Furthermore, the Antichrist will be very active during the movement of these various armies.

The confusion lies in the use of the word "battle" in Revelation 16:14 and other passages referring to Armageddon. The word should be translated "war." It is more than one battle; it is a series of battles, or a campaign. So the Battle of Armageddon is, in reality, a campaign or war which will extend over several years, and then reach a terrible climax. Once this truth about the word "battle" is seen, a great deal of confusion about Armageddon is resolved.

The last great war will involve many nations and will end in the decisive, final battle at Armageddon. The nations of the world will fight against God and His forces. The prophecies connected with this time indicate that God will come to the rescue of His people Israel on two separate occasions.

In Ezekiel 38:9 we read how the great hordes from the north, the land of Russia, come against Palestine: "Thou shalt ascend and come like a storm, thou shalt be like a cloud to cover the land, thou, and all thy bands, and many people with thee." Before this phase of the campaign is finished, it will bring war to the land of Palestine.

Four places mentioned in the Scriptures are connected with the war of Armageddon. First is Armageddon itself, which means "hill of Megiddo." Geographically, Megiddo is located on the southern rim of the plain of Esdraelon in the northern portion of Palestine. This was the great battlefield of Palestine. This plain, or valley, is 14 miles wide and 20 miles long and was thought by Napoleon to be the greatest site for warfare in the entire world. It is like a huge arena surrounded by mountains, but it is too small to accommodate the army of 200 million that is predicted to take part in the final battle of Armageddon.

A second area associated with Armageddon is the "valley of Jehoshaphat." The Book of Joel tells of this valley: "I will also gather all nations, and will bring them down into the valley of Jehoshaphat, and will plead with them there for my people and for my heritage Israel, whom they have scattered among the nations, and parted my land. ... Let the heathen be wakened, and come up to the valley of Jehoshaphat: for there will I sit to judge all the heathen round about" (3:2,12). The valley of Jehoshaphat is not the same as the valley of Armageddon, though some have confused the two. The valley of Jehoshaphat is near Jerusalem. It extends from east of Jerusalem across the Jordan River and then northward. It was a great trade route for centuries. Many great battles have also been fought in this particular area.

A third place associated with Armageddon is Idumea, which is another name for "Edom." Isaiah 34:6 tells of this place: "The sword of the Lord is filled with blood, it is made fat with fatness, and with the blood of lambs and goats, with the fat of the kidneys of rams: for the Lord hath a sacrifice in Bozrah, and a great slaughter in the land of Idumea." Edom is located southeast of Jerusalem and thus is separated from Megiddo by many miles.

Fourth, Jerusalem and Judah are specifically mentioned in connection with Armageddon. Zechariah 12:2 says, "Behold, I will make Jerusalem a cup of trembling unto all the people round about, when they shall be in the siege both against Judah and against Jerusalem." Later in the same book, God said through the Prophet

Zechariah, "For I will gather all nations against Jerusalem to battle [war]; and the city shall be taken, and the houses rifled, and the women ravished; and half of the city shall go forth into captivity, and the residue of the people shall not be cut off from the city" (14:2).

Thus we see that four different localities are identified with the great war of Armageddon—the valley of Megiddo in the north, the valley of Jehoshaphat east of Jerusalem, Idumea, or Edom, to the southeast, and Judah and Jerusalem.

The following description is given of the last great battle of Armageddon: "And the angel thrust in his sickle into the earth, and gathered the vine of the earth, and cast it into the great winepress of the wrath of God. And the winepress was trodden without the city, and blood came out of the winepress, even unto the horse bridles, by the space of a thousand and six hundred furlongs" (Rev. 14:19,20).

Never has there been a war in history like this will be. Hundreds of millions of men from all nations of the earth will fight against the armies of heaven. But the outcome will not be in doubt for a moment. The rebellion of the nations against God will be completely crushed.

Chapter 10

Four Confederations of Nations

It is important to identify the four groups, or confederations, of nations that will be on earth during the Tribulation. One will come from the old Roman Empire, as indicated by the ten toes of Nebuchadnezzar's dream image (Dan. 2:42,43) and the ten horns of Daniel's vision (7:7,8). This will be the western confederation. After the Church has been taken from the earth before the Tribulation begins, the western confederation, with the Antichrist as its leader, will appear on the scene. Possibly that which will unify the nations in this confederation will be their fear of the Communist countries to the north.

The Antichrist, as indicated in Daniel 9:27, will make a covenant with Israel, thereby offering the nation protection. From A.D. 70, when the Romans completely destroyed Jerusalem and scattered the Israelites, until 1948 there was no possibility of such a covenant's being made with Israel. Now there is that possibility.

Isaiah warned the people concerning this covenant, calling it a covenant with death, and with hell (Isa. 28:14-18). Israel will put her trust in the Antichrist, but God calls their agreement a covenant with hell. The Israelites will make lies their refuge; they will hide themselves under falsehoods. Because of this, God says, "Behold, I

79

lay in Zion for a foundation a stone, a tried stone, a precious corner stone, a sure foundation: he that believeth shall not make haste" (v. 16). This verse emphasizes that those who trust in the true Messiah—Christ—will not hurry to endorse the covenant with the Antichrist. Among the believing Israelites will be the 144,000, whose sealing is recorded in Revelation 7:4-8. They will form a believing remnant who will have no part in the covenant with the Antichrist.

In Isaiah 28:17,18 the Lord warns Israel that her covenant with the Antichrist will not stand. God says, "Your agreement with hell shall not stand; when the overflowing scourge shall pass through, then ye shall be trodden down by it" (v. 18).

A second great political power is called "the king of the north" (Dan. 11:6). This refers to the great Russian confederacy with its allies, including some nations of the Middle East.

A third group is called "the king of the south" (Dan. 11:9), which refers to Egypt and its allies.

A fourth great power is referred to in Daniel 11:44 and Revelation 16:12. This confederation is made up of "the kings of the east" who come from beyond the Euphrates River. In Daniel 11 all four of these groups are brought together as the war, or campaign, of Armageddon progresses.

This campaign will probably begin shortly after the Antichrist makes his agreement with Israel and begins to take on stature as a leading ruler. Then the king of the south—Egypt and her allies—will come against him. It appears that only a spark is needed to ignite the entire Middle East into war.

The conditions of the world make these final events seem very near.

The particular movement spoken of in Daniel 11:40 has to do with the actions of the king of the south against Palestine: "And at the time of the end shall the king of the south push at him: and the king of the north shall come against him like a whirlwind, with chariots, and with horsemen, and with many ships; and he shall enter into the countries, and shall overflow and pass over." At about the same time, the king of the north will move down with his armies. Their object will be to destroy Israel, but they will have to fight the Antichrist before they can do so, for he will have become Israel's protector by covenant.

When Gog, the king of the north, comes against Israel, God will unleash His fury against the foes of Israel. God says of that time, "My fury shall come up in my face. For in my jealousy and in the fire of my wrath have I spoken, Surely in that day there shall be a great shaking in the land of Israel" (Ezek. 38:18,19).

God will start fighting for His people with a great earthquake as a prelude to other judgments: "So that the fishes of the sea, and the fowls of the heaven, and the beasts of the field, and all creeping things that creep upon the earth, and all the men that are upon the face of the earth, shall shake at my presence, and the mountains shall be thrown down, and the steep places shall fall, and every wall shall fall to the ground. And I will call for a sword against him throughout all my mountains, saith the Lord God: every man's sword shall be against his brother. And I will plead against him with pestilence and with blood; and I will rain upon

81

him, and upon his bands, and upon the many people that are with him, an overflowing rain, and great hailstones, fire, and brimstone. Thus will I magnify myself, and sanctify myself; and I will be known in the eyes of many nations, and they shall know that I am the Lord" (vv. 20-23).

In Ezekiel 39 God tells how He will destroy the confederation from the north, leaving a sixth of the army to return to their land. This battle will be the first in a series in the war of Armageddon; and God will use such things as hail, fire, rain and pestilence to defeat the huge army from the north.

After God's destruction of the southern and northern powers, the Antichrist will begin to conquer more territory, though Edom and Moab and some other areas will escape seizure. Daniel 11:41 says, "He shall enter also into the glorious land, and many countries shall be overthrown: but these shall escape out of his hand, even Edom, and Moab, and the chief of the children of Ammon." About this time, also, the Antichrist will break his covenant with Israel and establish a system of worship with himself as God and with his own image in the temple (II Thess. 2:4). The presence of the image in the temple is referred to in the Scriptures as the "abomination of desolation" (Dan. 9:27; 12:11; Matt. 24:15).

The Antichrist will also move into northern Africa: "He shall stretch forth his hand also upon the countries: and the land of Egypt shall not escape. But he shall have power over the treasures of gold and of silver, and over all the precious things of Egypt: and the Libyans and the Ethiopians shall be at his steps" (Dan. 11:42,43). Though the Antichrist will seem to be victorious, his desecration of the temple and his control of Jerusalem will bring God's wrath on him.

The forces from the Far East will then begin to move toward the Promised Land: "But tidings out of the east and out of the north shall trouble him: therefore he shall go forth with great fury to destroy, and utterly to make away many" (11:44). Revelation 16:12 tells us how it is possible for the armies of the east to move into Palestine: "And the sixth angel poured out his vial upon the great river Euphrates; and the water thereof was dried up, that the way of the kings of the east might be prepared." This great natural barrier will be overcome and the nations will be brought together for the final showdown at Armageddon. When the Antichrist is in the midst of his conquest in Libya and Ethiopia, news from the east will cause him to return to Palestine ready to bring havoc and carnage.

The Far Eastern nations, the coalition of the Asiatic people, will have no intention of being ruled by the European confederation. Thus, a huge army of 200 million will come from the east across the dry Euphrates riverbed to the land of Palestine (Rev. 9:13-16).

By this time, preparations for war will have again been made in the north, because we are told that the Antichrist will hear news not only out of the east but also "out of the north" (Dan. 11:44). The "north" here refers to either the regrouping of the forces of Russia or, more probably, the country of Syria, north of Palestine. The movement of these forces from the north and the east into the land will set the stage for the final climactic battle of the great campaign of Armageddon.

While the armies from the east and the north are converging on Palestine, the Antichrist will return from northern Africa "with great fury to destroy, and utterly to make away many" (v. 44). The Antichrist will be indwelt by Satan, and in his insane desire for power, he will feel he can conquer anything and everything.

Then we are told that the Antichrist "shall plant the tabernacles of his palace between the seas in the glorious holy mountain; yet he shall come to his end, and none shall help him" (v. 45). "Between the seas" is a reference to the Mediterranean Sea and the Dead Sea. "The glorious holy mountain" refers to the Jerusalem area. Therefore, we see that the Antichrist will make the area in and around Jerusalem the base of his operations.

Concerning this time, God said in Zechariah 12:2,3, "Behold, I will make Jerusalem a cup of trembling unto all the people round about, when they shall be in the siege both against Judah and against Jerusalem. And in that day will I make Jerusalem a burdensome stone for all people: all that burden themselves with it shall be cut in pieces, though all the people of the earth be gathered together against it." What an amazing statement! Any nation or group of nations that attacks Israel in that day will find itself hurt by its very actions. It will be cut to pieces regardless of how large its armies may be.

According to Zechariah 14:1-3, God will bring the nations against Jerusalem and allow them to have partial victory over the city, and then He will bring His judgment on the oppressors. It is then that the Antichrist will come to his end and there will be none to help him. Satan's masterpiece, the Antichrist, will think he is able to conquer any force brought against him. But at the climax of the great campaign of Armageddon he will be utterly defeated.

We learn from Revelation 19 that there will be an invasion of Palestine from still another quarter. It will not be from the earth but from outer space—not from Mars but from heaven itself: "And I saw heaven opened, and behold a white horse; and he that sat upon him was called Faithful and True, and in righteousness he doth judge and make war. His eyes were as a flame of fire, and on his head were many crowns; and he had a name written, that no man knew, but he himself. And he was clothed with a vesture dipped in blood: and his name is called The Word of God. And the armies which were in heaven followed him upon white horses, clothed in fine linen, white and clean. And out of his mouth goeth a sharp sword, that with it he should smite the nations: and he shall rule them with a rod of iron: and he treadeth the winepress of the fierceness and wrath of Almighty God. And he hath on his vesture and on his thigh a name written, King of Kings, and Lord of Lords" (vv. 11-16).

The warring Gentile nations will suddenly forget their hostility and animosity toward each other and will turn against the Lord Himself. Thus we are told: "And I saw the beast, and the kings of the earth, and their armies, gathered together to make war against him that sat on the horse, and against his army" (v. 19). The audacity and

85

insanity of man to think that he can fight heaven itself! The several hundred million soldiers will be destroyed because out of the mouth of the Lord will come a sharp sword with which He will smite them. As in His creative acts, Christ has simply to speak the word—the sword of His mouth—and the armies will be destroyed.

Apparently, Satan thinks that by gathering all humanity together he can prevent the return of the Lord Jesus Christ. But the very size of Satan's forces only serves to demonstrate how weak they really are in comparison to the power of Christ. The armies will be destroyed and then the two key leaders through whom Satan will work during the Tribulation—the Antichrist and the false prophet—experience final judgment also. The Apostle John continued in Revelation: "The beast was taken, and with him the false prophet that wrought miracles before him, with which he deceived them that had received the mark of the beast, and them that worshipped his image. These both were cast alive into a lake of fire burning with brimstone" (v. 20). This is God's program, and it will not fail.

Chapter 11

The Final Invitation

"And at that time shall Michael stand up, the great prince which standeth for the children of thy people and there shall be a time of trouble, such as never was since there was a nation even to that same time: and at that time thy people shall be delivered, every one that shall be found written in the book. And many of them that sleep in the dust of the earth shall awake, some to everlasting life, and some to shame and everlasting contempt" (Dan. 12:1,2). These two verses summarize the prophetic statements in Daniel which relate to the end times. They also form a summary of Revelation 4—21.

Michael, the archangel, who is called here "the great prince," will be the great defender of the people of Israel. He has a great army of heavenly beings at his command to carry out the purposes of God.

Announcing different parts of God's program seems to be one of the angel Gabriel's special duties. It was probably Gabriel who announced the birth of Christ to the shepherds on the first Christmas. Certainly it was Gabriel who appeared to Mary. Michael, on the other hand, is the great warrior. Michael will defend God's people during the time of national and international evil and judgment that is to come.

A passage which parallels Daniel 12:1,2 is Revelation 12:7-10: "And there was war in heaven: Michael and his angels fought against the dragon; and the dragon fought and his angels, and prevailed not; neither was their place found any more in heaven. And the great dragon was cast out, that old serpent, called the Devil, and Satan, which deceiveth the whole world: he was cast out into the earth, and his angels were cast out with him. And I heard a loud voice saying in heaven, Now is come salvation, and strength, and the kingdom of our God, and the power of his Christ: for the accuser of our brethren is cast down, which accused them before our God day and night."

Though blessing results from Satan's being cast out of heaven, there will be trouble on the earth. Verse 12 says, "Woe to the inhabiters of the earth and of the sea! For the devil is come down unto you, having great wrath, because he knoweth that he hath but a short time." Satan will have only three and a half years left to try to accomplish his purposes, so he will initiate a program of hate and persecution—particularly against Israel.

In spite of the worst that Satan can do, God's redemptive program will continue. Daniel 12 indicates that the Old Testament saints will be resurrected at the end of the Tribulation. Verse 1 speaks of the "time of trouble, such as never was since there was a nation even to that same time." This is a reference to the last part of the Tribulation. Verses 2 and 3 tell of the resurrection of the Old Testament saints. On the surface, verse 2 seems to indicate that both the saved and the unsaved will be resurrected at this time. However, a more literal translation of this verse would be

"And many shall awake out from among the sleepers in the earth dust. These shall be unto life everlasting but those shall be unto shame and contempt everlasting." "These" refers to the ones who awake, whereas "those" refers to the ones who do not awake at that time. It is a characteristic of Old Testament Scriptures to group together events that are separated by years. For example, Isaiah 9:6 speaks of both the first and second comings of Christ when it says, "For unto us a child is born, . . . and the government shall be upon his shoulder."

Another indication that the resurrection of Old Testament saints follows the Tribulation is found in Daniel 12:11,12, which mentions two time periods—of 1290 and 1335 days. Half of the Tribulation, or three and one-half years, is customarily referred to as 1260 days. Since the last half of the Tribulation is being referred to in this portion of Daniel, it is obvious that these extra days extend beyond the Tribulation itself. Whatever the reason for the 75 extra days, it is clear that the time referred to is after the Tribulation. Then Daniel was told, "But go thou thy way till the end be: for thou shalt rest, and stand in thy lot at the end of the days" (v. 13). This seems to be an indication that Daniel would not be resurrected until after the Tribulation.

Nowhere, apart from passages dealing with the Church, do the Scriptures indicate a mass resurrection of the believers before the Tribulation.

Believers who are part of the Body of Christ, the Church, are "in Christ." These believers will be raptured from the earth before the Tribulation begins. This event is referred to in I Thessalonians

89

4:16,17: "For the Lord himself shall descend from heaven with a shout, with the voice of the archangel, and with the trump of God: and the dead in Christ shall rise first: then we which are alive and remain shall be caught up together with them in the clouds, to meet the Lord in the air: and so shall we ever be with the Lord."

Because many of these truths would not be clear until the New Testament prophecies were given, Daniel was told, "But thou, O Daniel, shut up the words, and seal the book, even to the time of the end" (Dan. 12:4). We are living in or near the end time. God told Daniel that in the end time "many shall run to and fro, and knowledge shall be increased" (v. 4). The *Berkeley Version* translates this phrase: "Many shall investigate and information shall advance." In other words, at the end time there will be more knowledge of the meaning of events in Daniel's prophecy.

Notice that both Daniel 12 and I Thessalonians 4 mention the presence of an archangel. In Daniel 12 we are told that Michael will stand up for the children of Israel. First Thessalonians 4 states that the voice of the archangel will be heard when the Church saints are called into the presence of the Lord Jesus Christ.

We learn of the resurrection of the martyred saints of the Tribulation through reading what the Apostle John wrote in Revelation 20:4: "I saw the souls of them that were beheaded for the witness of Jesus, and for the word of God, and which had not worshipped the beast, neither his image, neither had received his mark upon their foreheads, or in their hands; and they lived and reigned with Christ a thousand years." Many persons will be born again during the Tribulation—both Jews and Gentiles. Those who give their lives for their faith during the Tribulation will be resurrected at the end of the seven years when the Old Testament saints are also resurrected. This is the third part of the first resurrection.

The Scriptures refer to two resurrections—the "resurrection of life" and the "resurrection of damnation" (John 5:29). Revelation 20:5,6 refers to these resurrections as the "first resurrection" and the "second death."

There are several stages in the resurrection of life. First Corinthians 15 makes this clear when it says, "For as in Adam all die, even so in Christ shall all be made alive. But every man in his own order: Christ the firstfruits; afterward they that are Christ's at his coming. Then cometh the end, when he shall have delivered up the kingdom to God, even the Father; when he shall have put down all rule and all authority and power" (vv. 22-24). The resurrection of Christ was the first stage of the first resurrection. Second is the resurrection of the Church saints at the time of the Rapture. The third stage of the first resurrection includes the Old Testament saints as well as the resurrection of the Tribulation saints.

After Daniel heard the things recorded in chapter 12 of his book, he confessed, "I heard, but I understood not: then said I, O my Lord, what shall be the end of these things? And he said, Go thy way, Daniel: for the words are closed up and sealed till the time of the end" (vv. 8,9). God assured Daniel that "many shall be purified, and made white, and tried; but the wicked shall do wickedly: and none of the wicked shall understand; but the wise shall understand" (v. 10).

The unbelievers—those who have not placed their faith in the Lord Jesus Christ—cannot understand these prophecies. God reveals them only to His own people. In His final message to Daniel, God said, "But go thou thy way till the end be: for thou shalt rest, and stand in thy lot at the end of the days" (v. 13). God has a special place for Daniel as well as for all who die in the Lord. God has no pleasure in the wicked at any time, but He offers salvation to all in this life. This invitation should not be considered lightly or ignored.

The Bible warns us to watch because we do not know when the Lord will come. We must prepare now to meet Him because it will be too late to get ready if we wait until we hear the voice of the archangel and the trumpet of God. In fact, no one has a guarantee that he will live until that time. The only time we can be sure of is now. Second Corinthians 6:2 emphasizes this: "Now is the accepted time; behold, now is the day of salvation."

The five foolish virgins of Matthew 25 illustrate the fallacy of waiting until the Lord appears to prepare for Him. These virgins represent the Israelites on earth at the end of the Tribulation. While some of the nation will be prepared to meet the Lord when He returns to earth, some will be foolish and unprepared. Those who are ready will be able to enter the Millennium with the Lord. Those who are unprepared will be told, as were the five foolish virgins, "Verily I say unto you, I know you not" (v. 12).

The Rapture may take place at any time. Are

you ready to meet the Lord if He should appear today? You can be ready by receiving Jesus Christ as your personal Saviour. The Word of God promises, "As many as received him, to them gave he power to become the sons of God, even to them that believe on his name" (John 1:12).